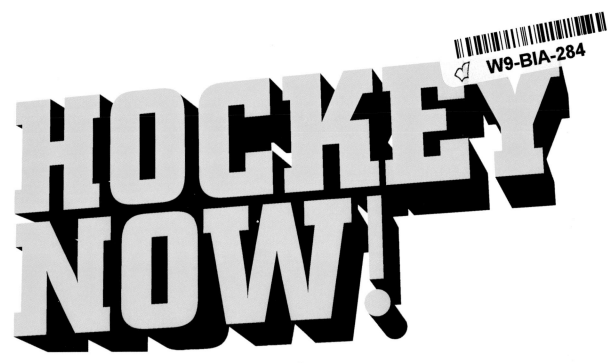

HOCKEY NOW!

NINTH EDITION

THE BIGGEST STARS OF THE NHL

MIKE RYAN

FIREFLY BOOKS

A Firefly Book

Published by Firefly Books Ltd. 2017

First printing

Publisher Cataloging-in-Publication Data (U.S.)
Names: Ryan, Mike, 1974-, author.
Title: Hockey Now! : The Biggest Stars of the NHL / Mike Ryan.
Description: Richmond Hill, Ontario, Canada : Firefly Books, 2017. | Ninth Edition.
    | Includes index. | Summary: "Hockey Now! features profiles and full-color images
    of over 70 star players in the NHL today. The book is divided by division, and each
    division features first and second star teams selected by the author as well as black
    aces and milestone veterans" -- Provided by publisher.
Identifiers: ISBN 978-1-77085-958-6 (paperback)
Subjects: LCSH: National Hockey League -- Biography. | Hockey players – Biography.
    | BISAC: SPORTS & RECREATION / Hockey. | BIOGRAPHY &
    AUTOBIOGRAPHY / Sports.
Classification: LCC GV848.5.A1R936 |DDC 796.9620922 – dc23

Library and Archives Canada Cataloguing in Publication
Ryan, Mike, 1974-, author
        Hockey now! : the biggest stars of the NHL / Mike
Ryan. -- Ninth edition.

Includes index.
First-Eighth editions by Mike Leonetti.
ISBN 978-1-77085-958-6 (softcover)

        1. Hockey players--Biography. 2. National Hockey
League--Biography. 3. Hockey players--Pictorial works.
4. National Hockey League--Pictorial works. I. Leonetti, Mike,
1958- . Hockey now! II. Title. III. Title: Biggest stars of the
National Hockey League.

GV848.5.A1L455 2017   796.962092'2   C2017-904610-1

Published in the United States by
Firefly Books (U.S.) Inc.
P.O. Box 1338, Ellicott Station
Buffalo, New York 14205

Published in Canada by
Firefly Books Ltd.
50 Staples Avenue, Unit 1
Richmond Hill, Ontario L4B 0A7

Cover and interior design: Kimberley Young

Printed in Canada

Canada [*] We acknowledge the financial support of the Government of Canada.

This book is dedicated to the memory of Mike Leonetti, who left big skates to fill with the *Hockey Now!* franchise, and Aaron Costescu, a kind soul and a far better athlete than me.

TABLE OF CONTENTS

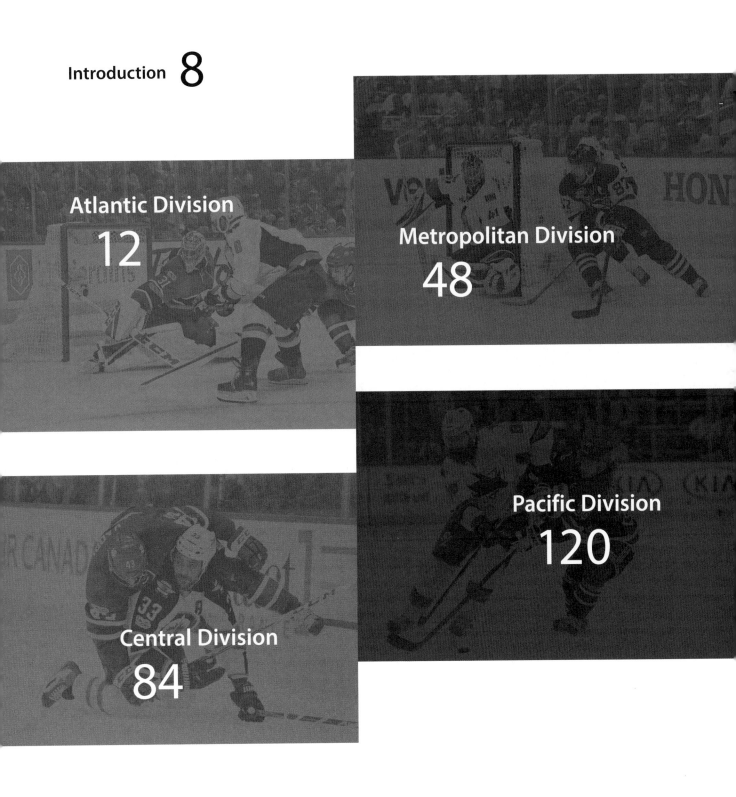

'd first like to recognize Mike Leonetti, the architect and author of the previous editions of *Hockey Now!*, whom we lost in 2016. To paraphrase the line in John McRae's "In Flanders Fields" that continues to inspire the Montreal Canadiens from their dressing room wall, with great respect I'll take the torch and try to hold it high.

Mr. Leonetti was writing about hockey when I was still sending away for the last few players to complete my NHL sticker books. I'd take the stickers and create dream lineups on my bedroom floor with my favorite players before affixing them in their places. Those books and my fantasy teams were the inspiration for this edition. After some fierce internal debate and shuffling as the season played out, I put my chosen players from all four NHL divisions into three tiers: "First Stars," "Second Stars" and "Black Aces." These days I'm still in awe of the NHL's best, but I'm much more objective in ranking them.

The NHL likes a good list, too, and in January 2017 the league announced the 100 Greatest NHL Players as part of its centennial celebrations. Six active players made it, including three Blackhawks — Patrick Kane, Duncan Keith and Jonathan Toews — which is why the Nashville Predators' sweep of Chicago on their way to the 2017 Stanley Cup Final was such a surprise. That run made Smashville the place to be in the spring, while Canadiens fans were left conflicted as they watched P.K. Subban get close enough to smell the Cup.

The mysterious alchemy for NHL success is beyond my comprehension, but it's something that Pittsburgh Penguins management has figured out with the first back-to-back Stanley Cups in the salary cap era. Some of that is down to Sidney Crosby and Evgeni Malkin, of course, and the latter was noticeably absent from the NHL's top 100 list. Often overlooked because of his teammate, Malkin was moved from Second Star to First Star after I took a closer look at his stats, accomplishments and highlights, which are already Hall of Fame-worthy.

The other three active players on the all-time list are Jaromir Jagr, Alex Ovechkin and Crosby. Jagr is the grand old man of the game and a player seemingly impervious to the ravages of time. He's featured in the "Milestones" — a section of each chapter where some of this generation's finest are lauded for hitting rare heights in the autumns of their careers. Ovechkin was a tap-in for both the NHL's 100 and my First Stars team. He recorded his 1,000th point in 2017, and a lack of playoff success doesn't change the fact that he's been the league's greatest goal-scorer for over a decade and one of the best in history. Crosby hit 1,000 points himself about a month later, and after earning his second Maurice Richard Trophy, he won his second-straight Conn Smythe Trophy in 2017. He's the first repeat winner since Penguins owner Mario Lemieux in 1991 and 1992. It cemented his status as the best player of his era, a crown he's not ready to relinquish yet, even if the NHL Awards were a coronation for Connor McDavid.

The next generation of players is as skilled and exciting as any in history, with McDavid leading the charge and the NHL with 100 points to win his first Art Ross Trophy. He also earned his first Hart Trophy in his second season, just like Crosby and Wayne Gretzky, who presented him with the MVP award. Fans in Edmonton can dare to dream of the Cup again with McDavid and Leon Draisaitl, just as Torontonians are looking forward to years of Calder Trophy winner Auston Matthews and his merry band of young Maple Leafs after decades in the wilderness.

But for every McDavid or Matthews (or Patrik Laine or Zach Werenski or Shayne Gostisbehere), there is a late bloomer. Players like Devan Dubnyk, Mark Giordano and 2017 Stanley Cup finalist Pekka Rinne had to fight doubts — both from management and within — to reach the top of the game. They give hope to young players who aren't being drafted high, or at all, and to a non-prodigy like me, who is easing deeper into his 40s. (For those scouts who may have lost their way, I play on weekends in

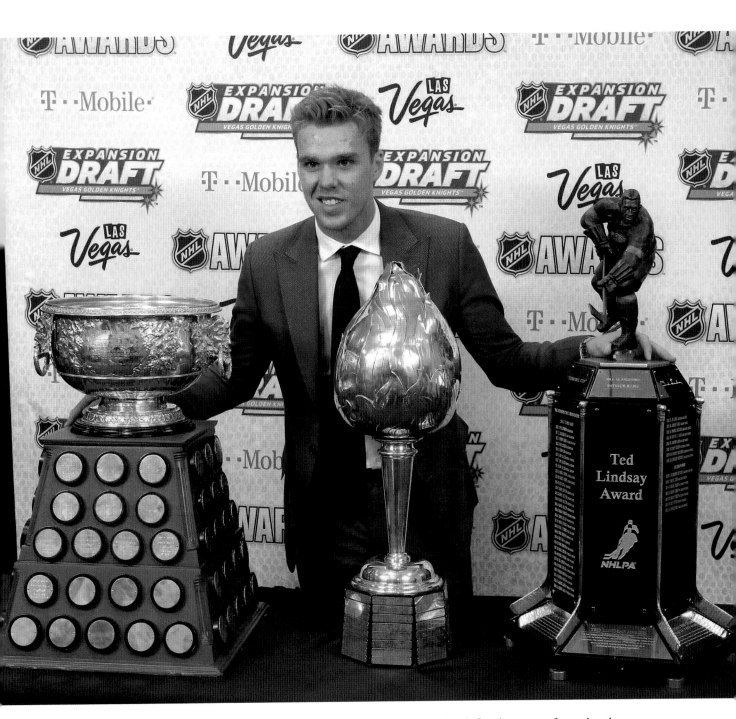

Toronto's DMHL and UUHA men's leagues.)

There are some lessons in these pages for up and coming players (and their eager parents). One is that many future NHL stars didn't play hockey in the summer. They took a healthy break to play other sports, such as baseball, lacrosse or soccer, which kept their passion for hockey alive. So many of these players have that passion in abundance — no one has to ask Crosby or McDavid to practice, it's all they want to do. They have a love for the game that borders on obsession.

I wrote this book for the young fans who share that obsession and for the older ones who remember studying their hockey cards and stickers with the same wonder I had. And if anyone disagrees with my selections, I'm always up for a healthy debate. That's half the fun of being a fan.

— Mike Ryan

ATLANTIC DIVISION

FIRST STARS

14	**PATRICE BERGERON**	Bruins	Center
16	**AUSTON MATTHEWS**	Maple Leafs	Center
18	**STEVEN STAMKOS**	Lightning	Center
20	**ERIK KARLSSON**	Senators	Defense
22	**SHEA WEBER**	Canadiens	Defense
24	**CAREY PRICE**	Canadiens	Goalie

SECOND STARS

26	**HENRIK ZETTERBERG**	Red Wings	Center
28	**BRAD MARCHAND**	Bruins	Left Wing
30	**MAX PACIORETTY**	Canadiens	Left Wing
32	**AARON EKBLAD**	Panthers	Defense
34	**VICTOR HEDMAN**	Lightning	Defense
36	**TUUKKA RASK**	Bruins	Goalie

BLACK ACES

38	**JACK EICHEL**	Sabres	Center
40	**NIKITA KUCHEROV**	Lightning	Right Wing
42	**MORGAN RIELLY**	Maple Leafs	Defense
44	**CRAIG ANDERSON**	Senators	Goalie

MILESTONES

| 46 | **JAROMIR JAGR** & **ROBERTO LUONGO** |
| | Panthers | Right Wing | Goalie |

PATRICE BERGERON

Won gold at the 2004 World Championship and 2005 World Juniors

Won gold at the 2010 and 2014 Olympics

Won the Stanley Cup in 2011

Awarded the Frank J. Selke Trophy four times (2012, 2014, 2015, 2017)

Won the 2016 World Cup of Hockey

orn in L'Ancienne-Lorette and raised in Charny, a suburb of Quebec City, Patrice Bergeron was a renaissance boy. But there was no doubt about his first love. "Hockey's his passion — it has always been his passion," according to Patrice's mother, Sylvie Bergeron-Cleary. "He was, I think, 10 years old when he was taking piano lessons. The instructor thought he was talented. Then one day he came home and said he wasn't going back."

The music teacher had suggested he give up hockey to play piano, so he quit piano.

Quitting hockey was never an option for Bergeron, even after being cut by the Seminary St.-François Blizzard Midget AAA team when he was in 10th grade. The following year Bergeron was named captain, and in his final year of high school he left home to play for the Acadie-Bathurst Titan in the Quebec Major Junior Hockey League.

Bergeron was drafted in the second round, 45th overall, by the Boston Bruins in 2003. He made his NHL debut as an 18-year-old, just three years after he couldn't make the Blizzard, and finished his rookie season with a gold medal at the 2004 World Championship. He then won gold for Canada at the 2005 World Juniors, making him the first player in history to win gold at the junior level after doing it with the senior team. He had 13 points in just six games and was named tournament MVP.

Bergeron was able to suit up for Canada as a junior player because NHLers were locked out in 2004–05. He was playing the season in the American Hockey League for the Providence Bruins when he left for the World Juniors. That's where Bergeron first made an impression on young prodigy Sidney Crosby. "I probably asked him about a thousand questions," recalled Crosby. "He was great about it, and we've been friends ever since."

The two have since shared a history of concussions. On October 27, 2007, Bergeron was checked from behind by Flyers defenseman Randy Jones. Knocked unconscious, he was taken from the arena

on a stretcher. Bergeron played 10 games in 2007–08 and missed a month the following season after sustaining a second concussion.

Back to full health in 2010, Bergeron added an Olympic gold to his World Championship and joined the ultra-exclusive Triple Gold Club with a Stanley Cup ring the following season. He had 20 points in 23 postseason games in 2011, including two goals in Game 7 as the Bruins beat the Vancouver Canucks to win their first championship in 39 years.

Bergeron led the NHL in 2011–12 with a plus-36 rating, was second in faceoff percentage (59.3) and won his first Selke Trophy as the best defensive forward in the league.

In 2013 the Bruins came within two wins of a second Stanley Cup with Bergeron playing through broken ribs and a punctured lung in the final. Immediately after losing Game 6 and the Cup to the Chicago Blackhawks, he was rushed to the hospital.

"I'd do it again because I had learned from others the sacrifices you need to make as a team in order to win in the playoffs," wrote Bergeron in The Players' Tribune in 2017. "I'd do it again because my teammates and I knew what it felt like to hoist the Cup."

Bergeron added a second gold medal at the 2014 Sochi Olympics and three more Selke Trophies in 2014, 2015 and 2017. He also became a charter member of the Quadruple Gold Club, teaming up with Crosby and fellow Bruin Brad Marchand on Canada's top line to score a combined 12 goals in six games and win the title at the 2016 World Cup of Hockey. Bergeron tied the final game with less than three minutes left before Marchand scored the winner.

Marchand saw his teammate raise his game against the world's best: "I was in awe. He was on another level, and I said that to him. He was like a man among boys. It's a lot of fun to watch him play."

AUSTON MATTHEWS

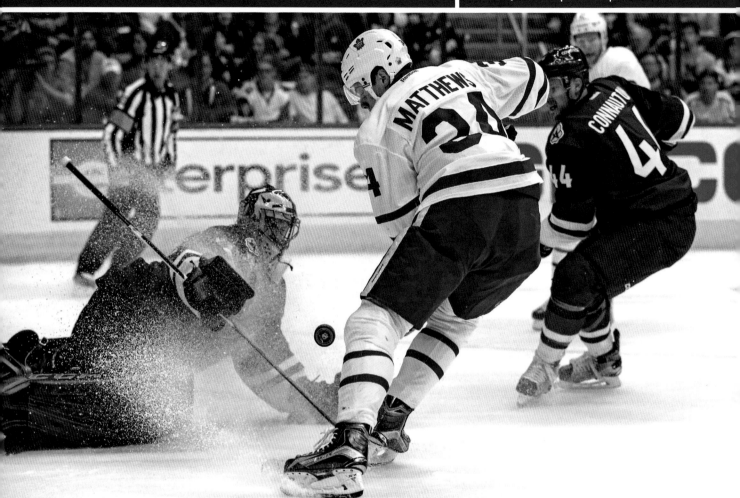

No NHL team is more thirsty for success than the Toronto Maple Leafs, who make a play-off appearance about as frequently as Halley's Comet is visible from Earth.

For the past 50 years, the Maple Leafs have been wandering in the championship desert in search of a Stanley Cup. But a savior arrived in 2016, from Arizona of all places, which is about as far away from Toronto as possible, in hockey terms.

Auston Matthews is a child of the NHL's southern expansion. He was raised in Scottsdale, Arizona, where he was seduced by the speed of Phoenix (now Arizona) Coyotes games.

Matthews learned the game on Ozzie Ice, a facility with two small rinks created by pipeline entrepreneur Dwayne Osadchuk. He played countless hours of 3-on-3 with older kids, and the quick, tight games forced him to learn to stickhandle in the proverbial phone booth. He also sharpened his skating under the unorthodox tutelage of Boris Dorozhenko, who fled the Soviet Union to run the Mexican national hockey team. Dorozhenko met Matthews' father, Brian, because they both spoke Spanish.

At 15 Matthews scored 55 goals and 100 points in 48 games with the AAA Arizona Bobcats, earning him a spot in the U.S. National Team Development Program. He played with the under-18 national team at 16, averaging nearly a point a game.

When Matthews was 17 he continued on the road less traveled, eschewing college or major junior hockey for a year in Europe. Two days shy of being eligible for the 2015 NHL entry draft, he chose to play in Zurich for the ZSC Lions in the National League A, Switzerland's top professional circuit.

Playing against men, the 18-year-old Matthews had 24 goals and 46 points in 36 games, the highest totals in league history for a player under 20. He won the Rising Star award and came second in MVP voting.

Meanwhile, in Toronto, the Maple Leafs had finished last in the NHL in 2015–16. The odds and draft lottery balls smiled upon them and they chose Matthews number one overall, their first top pick since they drafted Wendel Clark in 1985.

If there was any doubt Matthews could make it at the highest level he erased it in his first NHL game. On October 12, 2016, he had the greatest NHL debut in nearly 100 years.

Playing the Ottawa Senators, Matthews scored his first goal on his first shot less than nine minutes into his career. Later in the first period he stripped Norris Trophy winner Erik Karlsson to create his second goal, and early in the middle frame he became the first number one overall pick to have a hat trick in his debut. Then, with three seconds left in the second period, he became the first player in modern NHL history (since 1943–44) to score four goals in his first game. Only Joe Malone of the Montreal Canadiens and Harry Hyland of the Montreal Wanderers had more, both scoring five on December 19, 1917, the very first night of the newly formed NHL.

The cameras found Matthews' elated parents in the crowd. "Those were tears of joy," said his mother, Ema. "I feel very excited. This is what Auston has been dreaming since he was 6, [to] be playing right here in the NHL."

Brian echoed her sentiment: "I hope that nobody's going to wake me up here anytime soon. This is unbelievable."

The rest of the season was a dream for the Maple Leafs and Matthews. On March 7, 2017, he broke Clark's 31-year-old Maple Leafs rookie record with his 35th goal of the season, and on April 8 he scored his 40th into an empty net to clinch the Leafs' first playoff berth since 2013.

Matthews is the fourth player in NHL history to score 40 goals in a season before his 20th birthday, and he joined Mats Sundin as the only Leaf in the past 22 years to score at least 40. He also led the league in even-strength goals with 31 and was the only player in the league to record a shot in all 82 games. He capped his season by winning the Calder Trophy, becoming the first Leaf to be named rookie of the year since Brit Selby in 1966.

If the presumptive future captain raises the franchise's first Stanley Cup since 1967, the resulting celebrations just might blow Toronto off the map.

Selected first overall in the 2016 NHL entry draft

Scored four goals in his NHL debut, a first in the modern era

Played in the 2017 NHL All-Star Game

Won the Calder Trophy in 2017

STEVEN STAMKOS

Won gold at the 2008 World Juniors

Selected first overall in the 2008 NHL entry draft

Won the Maurice Richard Trophy twice (2010, 2012)

Played in four NHL All-Star Games (2010, 2012, 2015, 2016)

Won the 2016 World Cup of Hockey

f it weren't for bad luck, Steven Stamkos would have no luck at all.

The first-overall pick in 2008 by the Tampa Bay Lightning has lived up to his lofty status as one of the most natural goal scorers of his generation, but he's lost large swaths of his prime to injury.

Growing up in Unionville, Ontario, Stamkos played soccer and lacrosse and dreamed of being the Toronto Blue Jays' shortstop. He also started skating at two years old and played hockey with future NHL stars P.K. Subban and John Tavares.

Stamkos and Tavares played on a summer team together that went 50 games with one defeat, which Stamkos blames on reverse-favoritism. His father was the coach, but instead of sending out his son for the shootout he chose Tavares, who missed his attempt and cost them their unblemished record.

The two good friends became the second and third players, after Eric Lindros, to be drafted first over-all in both the Ontario Hockey League and NHL. Tavares was drafted a year earlier in the OHL because he'd been granted Exceptional Player Status, but Stamkos preceded him by a year in the NHL draft.

Stamkos earned his selection with big numbers for the Sarnia Sting, and he was also named the OHL's Scholastic Player of the Year. "He was an excellent student, an honor roll student. I could tell you that the teachers at our school were amazed at this kid," recalled Paul Titanic, Stamkos' coach on the Markham Waxers and gym teacher at St. Brother André Catholic School in Markham. "You'd expect this cocky kid coming back from Sarnia as the leading scorer in the OHL. But there'd be Steven, just trying to meld in and be part of the gang, doing his schoolwork to the best of his ability and never making excuses or asking for special consideration."

Stamkos made a good first impression in the NHL too. He won the Maurice "Rocket" Richard Trophy in his second season after leading the league with 51 goals in 2009–10. The following season he helped the Lightning reach the playoffs for the first time in

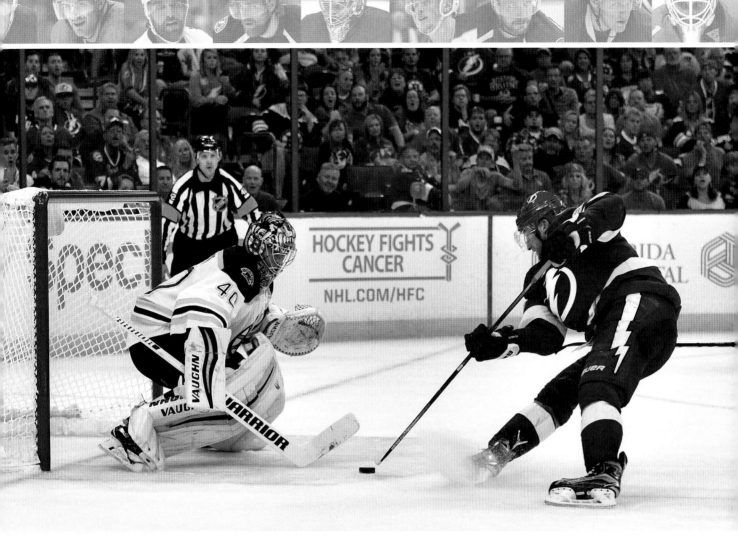

four years, where they lost the Eastern Conference Final in seven games to the Boston Bruins.

After dipping slightly to 45 goals in 2010–11 Stamkos became the second player since 1996 to score 60 goals the following season to win his second Maurice Richard Trophy.

Stamkos was skating smoothly toward Hall of Fame credentials, but injuries began taking their toll in 2013–14. He fractured the tibia in his right leg and missed 45 games. He returned on March 6, 2014, skating out for the first time as the captain of the Lightning, the 10th in franchise history.

After playing the full 82 games in 2014–15 and scoring 43 goals, Stamkos and the Lightning reached the Stanley Cup Final, losing in six games to the Chicago Blackhawks.

Tampa Bay was anticipating another long play-off run in 2015–16 when Stamkos was shut down with blood clots in his shoulder late in the season. He had a rib removed to alleviate the problem and

made an inspiring but ultimately futile comeback in the seventh game of the conference final against the Pittsburgh Penguins.

In a disturbing déjà vu, Stamkos had nine goals and 20 points in 17 games before tearing the lateral meniscus in his right knee in November 2016. He had surgery and missed the remainder of the season. Emotionally it was Stamkos' most difficult injury. "You just feel for him because you know how much he wants to play," said Lightning coach Jon Cooper.

"Stammer is in the prime of his career. He's one of the top goal-scorers. He's a dynamic player," said Steve Yzerman, the Lightning general manager and former Detroit Red Wing who was an inspiration for Stamkos growing up. "As you go through a season, it's nice to be able to look down the bench or look across the locker room and know that guy is going to make a difference here. We missed him a lot."

So did fans everywhere.

ERIK KARLSSON

When Erik Karlsson admitted to reporters during the 2017 playoffs that he had two hairline fractures in his left heel, he broke serious and longstanding protocol. The don't ask, don't tell policy for injuries in the postseason prevents your opponent from targeting your weakness, but as Karlsson said, "I'm not much for secrets."

In the Senators' Cinderella playoff run, opponents weren't going to slow Karlsson down anyway — he was their Achilles' heel.

Karlsson had been injured blocking a shot, an occupational hazard for a player with 201 blocks, the second most in 2016–17. His tendency to block might also be a result of his original desire to be a goalie, a notion his father crushed when he was 6.

Jonas Karlsson was a lumberjack in Landsbro in the south Swedish highlands and a defenseman in Sweden's top league, so when he dressed his son up in full goalie gear and wound up for a slap shot it scared young Erik right out of the net.

Playing defense, Karlsson was signed by Sodertalje SK when he was 16, but he was homesick and lasted only 10 games (getting 10 points) before joining Frolunda and winning Sweden's junior title in 2008.

Karlsson also played for Team Sweden and coach Anders Forsberg at the Under-18 World Championship in 2008. The Senators hired Forsberg as a scout soon after, and together with head scout Pierre Dorion they encouraged general manager Bryan Murray to move up in the 2008 entry draft to get him. At 5-foot-10, 157 pounds and looking like "a 12-year-old boy," according to Dorion, it took some convincing.

When Karlsson joined the Senators in 2009 his fluid skating and offensive acumen were obvious, but his defense and size were a work in progress. In 2011 then-coach Paul MacLean said Karlsson was capable of 30 minutes a night, as long as he's not "playing 14 minutes for us and 16 minutes for them."

It was a commentary on Karlsson's risk-taking playing style, which has produced some impressive numbers. In 2011–12, at 22 years old, he won his first Norris Trophy after his 78 points led all defensemen by a whopping 25. He was the second Swede to be named best defenseman, after Nicklas Lidstrom, one of his idols, and only the third player under 23, after Bobby Orr and Denis Potvin.

Karlsson was first among defensemen in points again in 2013–14 (74) and 2014–15 (66), when he won his second Norris Trophy. A third seemed likely in 2015–16 when he was first in the entire NHL in assists (66) and fourth in points (82) — the first time a defenseman had finished top-five in scoring since 1985–86. But he ended up losing to Drew Doughty, who had 31 fewer points.

Already one of the game's best defenseman, Karlsson showed he's one of the best leaders in the 2017 playoffs. He had 16 assists and 18 points in 19 games to take the Senators to the Eastern Conference Final. His two goals were both game-winners, and he had two defining moments.

In Game 2 of the first round against the Boston Bruins, cameras caught Karlsson yelling at teammate Derick Brassard. It was a rare moment of pique for the cool captain but a well-chosen one. Brassard tied the game in the third period, with a jaw-dropping assist from Karlsson, of course, before Ottawa won in overtime. "We looked at each other after the goal and we said, 'Are we good now, we good?'" laughed Brassard after the game.

In the next game Mike Hoffman scored on a breakaway after Karlsson sent a pass that traveled 116.3 feet, rose 10 feet in the air and landed on his tape. It was a breathtaking display of skill.

Karlsson had been an unstoppable force playing on one good foot, but the defending champion Pittsburgh Penguins proved to be an immovable object. A heartbreaking double-overtime loss in Game 7 of the East final spelled midnight for the Senators.

Still only 27, Karlsson was a finalist for the Norris Trophy once again in 2017. There is more hardware in Karlsson's future, and maybe even sainthood in Ottawa if it includes the Stanley Cup. "They always say God rested on the seventh day," said Dorion, now the Senators' general manager. "I think on the eighth day, he created Erik Karlsson."

Played in four NHL All-Star Games (2011, 2012, 2016, 2017)

Led all NHL defensemen in scoring four times (2011–12, 2013–14, 2014–15, 2015–16)

Won the Norris Trophy twice (2012, 2015)

Won silver at the 2014 Olympics and voted best defenseman

SHEA WEBER

Won gold at the 2005 World Juniors and 2007 World Championship

Played in six NHL All-Star Games (2009, 2011, 2012, 2015, 2016, 2017)

Won gold at the 2010 and 2014 Olympics

Received the Mark Messier Leadership Award in 2016

Won the 2016 World Cup of Hockey

S hea Weber is not a fan of the spotlight, but that wasn't a problem while he toiled in relative anonymity in Nashville. Yet that all changed with a seismic trade on June 29, 2016.

The Predators dealt Weber to the Montreal Canadiens for P.K. Subban, a swap of right-shooting defensemen in their prime, one with the biggest shot in the NHL, the other with the biggest personality. "I'm not P.K. Subban," said Weber after the trade. "I'm not going to try to be."

Which is why the Canadiens traded for him. Weber, who was the Predators' captain and the 2016 Mark Messier Leadership Award winner is "quiet, succinct, stoic but polite," according to sports writer Bryan Mullen in *The Tennessean*, "whose slap shots rip twine, break bones and create myths."

That's not an exaggeration. At least four teammates have broken bones after being hit by a Weber slap shot, and he's won the hardest shot at the NHL All-Star skills competition three years running, topping out at over 108 miles per hour in 2015.

The myth went international when Weber ripped a puck through the twine against Germany at the 2010 Vancouver Olympics, which had to be reviewed in slow motion to be seen and confirmed.

Weber grew up in Sicamous, British Columbia, a mountain town of about 3,000 people. He inherited his work ethic from his parents, a sawmill worker and a hairdresser, and his intimidating stare came from his mom, Tracy, who died of cancer a few months after seeing her son win Olympic gold in Vancouver.

Between the ages of 14 and 15, Weber shot up from 5-foot-9 to 6-foot-2, but it wasn't enough to convince the Western Hockey League and so he went undrafted. The Kelowna Rockets signed him for the 2001–02 season as a 16-year-old, and the following year he led the team with 167 penalty minutes. The Predators liked his pluck and drafted him in the second round, 49th overall, in 2003. "He's just an impressive person, all the way from when he was young to when he left," said Marc Habscheid, who

coached Weber and Kelowna to a Memorial Cup title in 2004. "A great person and great teammate, very coachable and very accountable, and all the traits you want not only as a player, but even as your son."

After winning gold at the World Juniors in 2005, Weber joined the Predators full-time for the 2006–07 season. Over the next decade he was Nashville's foundation and one of the game's finest defenseman.

The 6-foot-4, 236-pound safety valve plays up to 30 minutes a night. His 183 goals since entering the league lead all NHL defensemen, and he's finished in the top four in Norris Trophy voting five times.

Weber is a steady, calming presence on the blue line and he's earned respect from friends and foes alike. The Los Angeles Kings' Mike Cammalleri touts his attributes: "size, strength, defense, physicality, can score, does it all at an elite level. It's also the personality. There's a calm, humble confidence there."

Weber added a second Olympic gold at the 2014 Sochi Games, and after the trade to Montreal he won the title at the 2016 World Cup of Hockey.

One year does not a trade make, but Weber won over Habs fans quickly by leading the Canadiens in points and the NHL in plus-minus early in the 2016–17 season, finishing with 42 points and a plus-20 rating in 78 games.

Montreal had a better regular season than the Predators, but if the ultimate metric is proximity to the Stanley Cup, then Nashville came out on top by reaching the final.

Undaunted by the fishbowl of Montreal, Weber is putting down roots. Married to his high school sweetheart, Bailey, their two young children are enrolled in bilingual daycare and he's taking French lessons.

Weber still "burns for the Stanley Cup," according to Blair Robinson, his Junior B coach. In a city that's occasionally set on fire during the playoffs, he fits right in.

CAREY PRICE

I n the cauldron of Montreal, Carey Price exudes a natural calm, like he's wearing the wide-open space of home, not the fabled jersey of the Canadiens.

Price was born in Vancouver but moved to Anahim Lake, a remote town in central British Columbia, when he was 3. He has Nuxalk and Southern Carrier Indigenous heritage, and his mother, Lynda, is the chief of the Ulkatcho First Nation and the first woman elected to the Union of BC Indian Chiefs' board of directors.

The goaltending genes came from his father, Jerry, an eighth-round pick of the Philadelphia Flyers in 1978 whose bad knees kept him from reaching the NHL. There were no rinks in Anahim Lake, so Jerry cleared a section of Corkscrew Creek that ran through their property to teach his son. At 9, Carey had outgrown the creek, but the closest team was in Williams Lake, 200 miles away. After making the eight-hour round trip one too many times, his father bought a small plane to cut down on the commute. Father and son speak fondly of the time spent together on those trips, which ended when Carey moved to Pasco, Washington, at 16 to play for the Tri-City Americans of the Western Hockey League.

Price was the seventh overall pick in the 2002 WHL draft and went fifth overall in the 2005 NHL entry draft, despite the Canadiens having a Vezina and Hart Trophy winner in Jose Theodore. Then-general manager Bob Gainey couldn't pass up a "thoroughbred."

After the Americans were eliminated in the 2007 WHL playoffs, Price joined Hamilton for the American Hockey League postseason and posted a .936 save percentage to lead the Bulldogs to the Calder Cup. It topped a season in which he'd also won gold at the 2007 World Junior Championship. Price became the first goalie to be named Canadian Hockey League Goaltender of the Year, World Juniors MVP and the Jack Butterfield Trophy winner as AHL playoff MVP in the same season.

Despite this pedigree Price wasn't anointed Montreal's starter immediately. In 2010 the Canadiens made a surprise run to the Eastern Conference Final thanks to goaltender Jaroslav Halak. Forced to choose between goalies in the off-season, Montreal management traded Halak, to the consternation of many.

In his first preseason as the number one goalie, and with a brand new contract in his back pocket, Price had a shaky start and the fans let him know it. Afterward he counseled them to "relax, chill out."

That kind of calm is particularly helpful when the whole country is watching. At the 2014 Sochi Olympics Price had a 0.59 goals-against average and .972 save percentage in five games — all victories that included a shutout streak of 164:19 that stretched over the semifinal and gold medal game.

That was merely a prelude to a historic 2014–15 season. Price's league leading 44 wins broke a franchise record, and he was first in goals-against average (1.96) and save percentage (.933). He won the Hart Trophy, Vezina Trophy and Ted Lindsay Award — the first goalie to win all three — and shared the William Jennings Trophy with the Chicago Blackhawks' Corey Crawford.

During an acceptance speech, Price said, "I would really like to encourage First Nations youth to be leaders in their communities. Be proud of your heritage and don't be discouraged from the improbable."

A knee injury cost Price all but 12 games in 2015–16, but after rehabbing over the summer he returned to backstop Canada to victory at the 2016 World Cup of Hockey and was a Vezina finalist again in 2016–17.

After the Canadiens were eliminated in the first round of the 2017 playoffs, despite Price's 1.86 goals-against average and .933 save percentage, there were calls to trade him. With a year left on his contract it was a hysterical response in the era of instant analysis by media and fans alike.

But while that maelstrom swirled in Montreal, Carey and his family retreated to their off-season home in British Columbia, where they chill out. His patience paid off. Montreal wisely signed Price to an eight-year contract in the hopes that he'll bring the same success to the Canadiens as he has to Canada.

- Won gold at the 2007 World Junior Championship
- Played in five NHL All-Star Games (2008, 2011, 2012, 2015, 2017)
- Won gold at the 2014 Olympics and named best goaltender
- Won the Hart Trophy, Vezina Trophy, Ted Lindsay Award and William Jennings Trophy in 2015
- Won the 2016 World Cup of Hockey

HENRIK ZETTERBERG

The 2016–17 season was a dark one for the Detroit Red Wings. Franchise icon Gordie Howe and beloved owner Mike Illitch both died, and the season marked the end of both the Joe Louis Arena and the Wings' run of 25 straight play-offs appearances.

After a quarter-century of qualifying for the post-season, four Stanley Cups and a modern lineage that went from Steve Yzerman and Sergei Fedorov to Nicklas Lidstrom and Pavel Datsyuk, the Wings will be led by captain Henrik Zetterberg, the last ember of the dynasty, to their new digs in 2017–18.

One reason behind the Wings' sustained success had been their ability to unearth late round gems. Zetterberg was drafted in the seventh round, 210th overall, in 1999. After playing in the Swedish Elite League from 2000 to 2002 and on the 2002 Swedish Olympic team, he debuted in the NHL for the 2002–03 season. He scored 22 goals, had 22 assists and was runner-up in Calder Trophy voting. "From the day that he came into the organization, he was very mature and professional in the way he conducted himself on a daily basis," said Yzerman, former Wings' captain and now general manager of the Tampa Bay Lightning. "He has special qualities as a leader. He is a tremendous all-around player. From day one, he had all those abilities, which I really admire, because a lot of us had to learn all that stuff."

Zetterberg took an official leadership role in 2005–06 as an alternate captain and had his best season to date with 39 goals and 85 points in 77 games. He also won an Olympic gold and a World Championship in 2006, a rare double in one year.

In 2007–08, Zetterberg started the season by breaking a franchise record: he had at least one point in 17 straight games, surpassing the Red Wings record of 14 games set by Norm Ullman in 1960–61. He set career highs with 43 goals and 92 points and finished the season by joining the exclusive Triple Gold Club (players who have won a Stanley Cup, an Olympic gold medal and a World Championship).

Named to the NHL All-Rookie Team in 2003

Won gold at the 2006 Olympics and the 2006 World Championship

Won the Stanley Cup and Conn Smythe Trophy in 2008

Received the NHL Foundation Player Award in 2013

Won the King Clancy Award in 2015

In Game 6 of the 2008 Stanley Cup Final, Zetterberg scored the game-winner on Pittsburgh goalie Marc-Andre Fleury in the third period to give the Wings' their 11th Stanley Cup. It was his 13th goal and 27th point of the playoffs, which tied him with the Penguins' Sidney Crosby. He put on a master class at both ends of the ice to win the Conn Smythe as playoff MVP. "He is a Hall of Fame player," said Scotty Bowman, a former Wings coach and a Hall of Famer himself. "He is such a good two-way player. It's so reliable as a coach to have a guy like him, because you could play him against anybody. In 2008, he was going head-to-head against Sidney Crosby. Z was able to neutralize him."

Named Red Wings captain after Lidstrom retired in 2012, Zetterberg was also given the C for Sweden's 2014 Olympic team but had to pull out of the Games because of a back injury. After surgery to repair the damage and with him approaching his mid-30s, many thought the best days of his career were behind him. But Zetterberg's competitiveness and off-ice commitment to fitness and health have kept him among the game's elite. He led the Wings in scoring again in 2016–17 with 68 points.

On the last game of the regular season and the last to be played at the Joe, Zetterberg became the 54th player in NHL history to play 1,000 games with one franchise. He was the seventh player in club history, joining Howe, Lidstrom, Alex Delvecchio, Yzerman, Draper and Tomas Holmstrom.

As the team creates new memories at the Little Caesars Arena, one link to past glories remains. With four years left on his 12-year contract, the man with the impressive beard is not a relic in bronze just yet — he's the one to lead the young Wings to the start of a new playoff streak. But just getting there isn't enough. "There are a lot of great, great players who played for 15 years and haven't been in the Stanley Cup Final," said Zetterberg. "So just being a part of this is not the goal. The goal is to go all the way and win."

BRAD MARCHAND

Long known as the Little Ball of Hate, he's now one of the NHL's top scorers. And when it comes to Brad Marchand, you can't have the latter without the former.

Having made a name for himself as a troublemaker before he was a scorer, Marchand's moniker even caught the attention of the U.S. president. When Marchand was at the White House with his Boston Bruin teammates after winning the 2011 Stanley Cup, Barack Obama asked, "What's up with that nickname, man?" For once, Marchand was left speechless. "It really caught me off guard," he said. "I almost blacked out there [but] it was all in good fun."

The nickname was inherited from Pat Verbeek, who had 522 career goals and nearly 3,000 penalty minutes, but Marchand has been given plenty of his own; he's been called Squirrel, Weapon of Mass Distraction, Rat, Pigeon, Brat and Nose Face Killah. His first was Tomahawk, thanks to a two-handed swing that dented an opponent's facemask when he was a 14-year-old in Lower Sackville, Nova Scotia.

Rob O'Brien was in the stands scouting for his Dartmouth Subways major midget team when Marchand took batting practice on his opponent's face. It convinced him to recruit the undersized forward: "I really felt that his temperament could be an asset rather than a detriment. Brad is a real personality on the ice. A lot of coaches tried to beat that out of him, but I encouraged it. I thought it was fantastic that he was able to do it. I used it to his advantage."

After running roughshod with his midget team, Marchand was a second-round pick by the Moncton Wildcats in the 2004 Quebec Major Junior Hockey League draft. In 2006 Moncton reached the Memorial Cup final and soon after Boston drafted Marchand in the third round, 71st overall.

Marchand played two more seasons in junior, split between the Val-d'Or Foreurs and the Halifax Mooseheads, and won back-to-back gold medals at the World Juniors in 2007 and 2008 before turning pro. After a year and a half with the American Hockey League's Providence Bruins, he was called up to Boston midway through the 2009–10 season.

In his first full season the Bruins won their first Stanley Cup since 1972. Marchand had 11 goals in 25 playoff games in 2011, a Bruins rookie playoff record, and the team was 9-0 in games that he scored. He had five goals in the last five games against the Vancouver Canucks in the Stanley Cup Final, and also punched Canucks star Daniel Sedin in the jaw six times when the Bruins had Game 6 in hand. When asked why afterward, he replied, "Because I felt like it."

Marchand was penalized but escaped suspension. He scored two goals in the decisive seventh game, and he's been beloved in Beantown ever since.

In 2015–16 Marchand had 37 goals and a team-leading plus-21 rating. It earned him a spot on Team Canada for the 2016 World Championship, where he won gold. A few months later, he represented his country at the World Cup of Hockey. Playing alongside Sidney Crosby and Boston teammate Patrice Bergeron on Canada's top line, he led the tournament with five goals in six games. The coming-out party for the skilled agitator was capped with the winning goal, a shorthanded tally with less than a minute remaining.

Marchand signed an eight-year, $49 million contract with the Bruins the day before the World Cup final, some of which he's already given back to the league in fines.

There were two slewfoots in January 2017, one incurring a $10,000 fine and the other costing him $100,000 in salary, and he was suspended for the final two games of the regular season. But he also challenged for the NHL lead in goals and points, prompting Hart Trophy buzz. He finished tied for fourth in goals (39) and fifth in points (85), both career highs.

Marchand continues to light the lamp while living in the margins of the rulebook, because that's the fuel for his fire. "When people make reference to Brad's peskiness, I think they're misunderstanding it, actually," according to Marchand's father, Kevin. "I think what he's doing is applying his personality in different ways to gain inches on the ice, which are so critical because every inch leads to a goal scoring chance."

Won gold at the 2007 and 2008 World Junior Championships

Won the Stanley Cup in 2011

Led the NHL in shorthanded goals in 2013–14

Won the 2016 World Cup of Hockey and scored the winning goal

Played in the 2017 NHL All-Star Game

MAX PACIORETTY

Selected 22nd overall in the 2007 NHL entry draft

Awarded the Bill Masterton Trophy in 2012

Led the NHL in game-winning goals in 2013–14 with 11

Tied for the NHL lead in plus-minus in 2014–15 (plus-38)

There's no middle ground in Montreal — it's the Stanley Cup or bust. If you win, you're deified; if you lose, the ire of a city with a history of playoff rioting falls squarely on your shoulders, especially if you're the chosen leader.

Max Pacioretty was named the 29th captain of the Canadiens on September 18, 2015. Many expected it would be P.K. Subban — a charismatic presence in both the dressing room and the city. But the choice was made by the players, and rumor has it the vote wasn't close.

"Patches" wasn't preordained the way Maurice Richard or Jean Beliveau seemed to be sent by the Francophone hockey gods to lead the Canadiens. He was born in New Canaan, Connecticut, into a family that had little interest in hockey.

The Paciorettys' imaginations were first captured by Mark Messier's guaranteed win and the New York Rangers' Stanley Cup in 1994, and five-year-old Max took up the game — poorly at first, by his own admission. "My mom grew up in Mexico and had never been ice skating before in her life," recalled Pacioretty. "So I went out there the first time and I fell on my face and cut open my chin."

Undaunted, Pacioretty spent countless hours in the family's basement focusing on his now-lethal snapshot. Slowly, he began to show promise. When his mother realized he might have a future in hockey she subscribed to an NHL package to watch the game more, and her family started to call her "Donna Cherry."

In 2007 Pacioretty earned a scholarship to the University of Michigan and was drafted 22nd overall by the Canadiens. After one season as a Wolverine he split his first two pro seasons between Montreal and the American Hockey League's Hamilton Bulldogs. He scored on his first NHL shot on January 2, 2009.

Two years later, on March 8, 2011, Pacioretty was driven into the glass partition between the benches by 6-foot-9, 250-pound Zdeno Chara of the bitter rival Boston Bruins. The stomach-turning hit broke his neck. It led to a change in the configuration of

the glass, which is now rounded so players don't hit it flush, and to Pacioretty's other nickname, "Wolverine," a nod to both his alma mater and the Marvel Comic superhero known for his powers of recovery.

Back ahead of schedule for the 2011–12 season, Pacioretty had 33 goals and 65 points and won the Bill Masterton Trophy, given to the player who best exemplifies the qualities of perseverance, sportsmanship and dedication to the game.

Since 2011–12, only three players have scored more goals, just two have had more even-strength goals and Alex Ovechkin is the only player with more game-winners. Yet Pacioretty has never played in an All-Star Game and he's often been overshadowed by other Habs stars, including Shea Weber and Carey Price.

Pacioretty does get the criticism, however. He only had two goals in his first 14 games in 2016–17 and the knives came out. It was later revealed he was playing with a broken bone in his foot. But as he healed and the rest of the lineup was decimated by

injuries, he kept the Canadiens afloat.

Pacioretty scored 13 goals and 20 points in a 15-game stretch, including overtime winners in consecutive games. The second was his eighth overtime goal — setting a Canadiens career record — and the first back-to-back regular-season overtime winners in franchise history. Pacioretty finished the season tied for eighth in the NHL with 35 goals, his fourth season in a row with at least 30.

But it was all scorn and scrutiny in the 2017 playoffs after Pacioretty failed to score in a first-round loss to the Rangers. Fans' memories were short for the man who ensured they qualified for the postseason.

As Habs players past and present will testify, there's no better place to win than in Montreal and no tougher place to lose. Pacioretty has the demeanor to bear the weight of expectations from a fan base that believes the Stanley Cup is its birthright, but haven't seen one since 1993. He'll need it, the natives are getting restless.

AARON EKBLAD

Named OHL Rookie of the Year in 2012

Named the OHL's Most Outstanding Defenseman in 2014

Selected first overall in the 2014 NHL entry draft

Played in two NHL All-Star Games (2015, 2016)

Won the Calder Trophy in 2015

Aaron Ekblad has long been exceptional. In 2011, the Ontario Hockey League made it official, granting the 15-year-old Belle River, Ontario, native "Exceptional Player Status" so he could be drafted a year early. Already 6-foot-3 and 200-pounds, he had 34 points in 30 regular season games and 21 points in 18 playoff games for the Sun County Panthers minor midget team.

Ekblad was the first defenseman in the Canadian Hockey League to be given exceptional status, and the grateful Barrie Colts made him the first-overall pick in the OHL draft. It was not a mistake by league or franchise; he won the 2012 Emms Family Award as Rookie of the Year.

In his third and final OHL season Ekblad was named Most Outstanding Defenseman after 23 goals, 53 points and 91 penalty minutes in 58 regular season games. He also had seven goals and 17 points in the playoffs, with a plus-11 rating.

With scuttlebutt surrounding Ekblad and the first-overall pick in the upcoming entry draft, the 18-year-old responded with veteran savvy: "I'm a very calm person. Media and stuff like that, it's nothing I've ever not been through. It is what it is. It's the NHL draft. We've been preparing for this our whole lives. No one should be nervous here."

With the first pick in 2014 the Florida Panthers knew they had their man after interviewing Ekblad. "He just blew us out of the water, because his professionalism and maturity was incredible," said general manager Dale Tallon. "You go, this kid's not 18 years old or 17. He's 35. But he had a sparkle in his eye. He was sure of himself. He was a man-child for me. And I liked it."

Once again Ekblad proved he was worthy of his place in the draft. He had 12 goals and 39 points, the third-highest total by an 18-year-old defenseman in league history, behind Phil Housley and Bobby Orr, who also happens to be his agent. He was the first teenage blue-liner in five years to play more than 1,700 minutes, and he became the youngest defenseman to

win the Calder Trophy since Orr in 1967.

In his sophomore season Ekblad played in his second All-Star Game and the Panthers won the Atlantic Division. He signed an eight-year, $60 million contract and was named alternate captain prior to the 2016–17 season, but he got off to a slow start, and the Panthers slid out of playoff contention.

Ekblad has had to adjust to life without defense partner Brian Campbell and friend and former landlord Willie Mitchell, who both left the team, and a changing role from protégé to mentor to the young Panthers defense corps. According to Campbell, Florida has the right role model and one of the league's best. "What surprises me is how consistent he's been. This kid is above and beyond anything I would have expected. He's a special talent and it's fun to play with him. His hockey intelligence [is] really high … His points are good, but if he was on a team that strives to use its defense more in the offense, he

could be way up there."

Ekblad picked up his game in the second half of the season, but just as things were starting to look up he suffered a concussion. It was the third of his young career, and it followed either a mild concussion or whiplash (depending who you ask) that he sustained when he was playing for Team North America in the 2016 World Cup of Hockey. The Panthers shut him down for the last 14 games, protecting their most valuable asset.

Playing a position that takes most players years to master with a rare combination of size and skill, Ekblad has been called "perfect for the new NHL" by one scout, and Washington Capitals coach Barry Trotz says Ekblad has "Hall of Fame written all over him."

That's a few years off; just 21 at the start of his fourth NHL season in 2017–18 and showing his youth, Ekblad eats one cookie — but only one, he stresses — before every game.

VICTOR HEDMAN

When 18-year-old Victor Hedman joined the Tampa Bay Lightning after being drafted second overall in 2009, it was only the second team he'd ever played on. From the age of 6 he played in the legendary MoDo system in his hometown of Ornskoldsvik, Sweden. "Just a good hockey town, rinks everywhere, outdoor and indoor," said Hedman. "You're skating for hours and hours, you go home to eat and then you go out again. Get the lights on when it gets dark. Just all about hockey."

The main employer is paper mill Mo och Domsjo (now called Holmen), which sponsors MoDo and where Hedman's dad, Olle, worked when he wasn't managing equipment for the hockey team. The town of just 27,000 people that sits six hours north

of Stockholm has produced NHL stars Markus Naslund, Henrik and Daniel Sedin, and Hedman's favorite, Peter Forsberg, among many others. "It's just incredible," said Hedman of the number of NHL players who have come out of Ornskoldsvik. "When you look back on it, to have that childhood and that opportunity to play in that town, the heritage that you had growing up, it's pretty incredible to be at this stage now. It's something that I really appreciate."

Between organized and impromptu hockey and the bandy — a hockey/soccer hybrid — he played on the frozen fields around town, Hedman learned to skate through his awkward phases as he grew into his 6-foot-6 frame. Gawky growing up, the defenseman is now 223 pounds and one of the smoothest skaters in the NHL. "I don't know if fans really have an appreciation for it," said former teammate Matt Carle. "Because his legs are so long, his feet aren't moving as quick, but he is flying out there. You can see it when he's skating by people."

After winning silver medals with Sweden at the World Juniors in 2008 and 2009 and Rookie of the Year in the Swedish Elite League in 2009, the teenager made the move to Florida. "It's probably the toughest position to come into this league as an 18-year-old defenseman," said Lightning captain Steven Stamkos, who was drafted first overall by Tampa Bay the year before Hedman. "There were some tough years, but we went through tough years as a team."

Hedman, like Stamkos, had to learn from the press box as a healthy scratch early in his career, but both are now established stars and the fortunes of the Lightning have followed.

Tampa Bay reached the Eastern Conference Final in 2011, but Hedman struggled with injuries the following season and the team slipped back. Meanwhile, the Ottawa Senators' Erik Karlsson, a Swede born the same year as Hedman, won the Norris Trophy in 2012.

Hedman made his case for best defenseman in the game in the 2015 playoffs. Averaging 26 minutes a night and shutting down Jonathan Toews in the Stanley Cup Final, Hedman was a strong Conn Smythe candidate, but Tampa Bay fell to the Chicago Blackhawks in six games.

In 2016–17, Hedman led all defensemen and was fourth in the NHL with a career best 56 assists in 79 games. He had career highs in goals (16) and points (72), behind only Brent Burns of the San Jose Sharks among defensemen. He also led the NHL with 29 power-play assists and ranked second with 33 power-play points.

If it wasn't for career seasons by Burns and Karlsson, who joined Hedman as 2017 Norris Trophy finalists, and the fact that the injury-decimated Lightning missed the playoffs, he likely would have been crowned the NHL's best defenseman.

Hedman has taken his place in the pantheon of Ornskoldsvik role models and legends, only a few years removed from being an awestruck sophomore sharing the ice with the Sedins in Vancouver as Naslund's jersey was retired. "Can you believe it?" wrote Hedman in The Players' Tribune. "Four guys from the same small town in Sweden, all standing on NHL ice, watching Markus' jersey go up into the rafters. Amazing.

"When we caught up after the game, the talk was not about hockey. Naturally, it was, 'How is your father?' They wanted to know how my dad, the man who worked for MoDo for 20 years, was doing. Very Swedish."

Named Swedish Elite League Rookie of the Year in 2009

Awarded the Guldpucken (Golden Puck) as Sweden's best hockey player in 2015

Played in the 2017 NHL All-Star Game

Voted a finalist for the Norris Trophy in 2017

Won gold at the 2017 World Championship

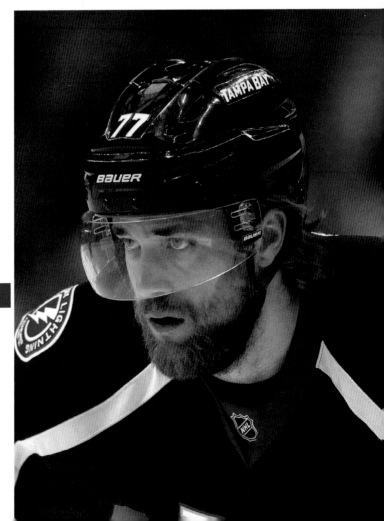

TUUKKA RASK

The Toronto Maple Leafs have made some questionable trades in their long history, but their 2006 acquisition of goaltender Andrew Raycroft from the Boston Bruins for Tuukka Rask really hurt them, and the pain lingers.

In fairness to then-Maple Leafs general manager John Ferguson Jr., Raycroft had won the Calder Trophy two years earlier and Toronto had both Rask and Justin Pogge, who had just backstopped Canada to gold at the World Juniors.

Finland took bronze at the same tournament and Rask was named Best Goalkeeper, but Ferguson told senior staff, "We'd get killed for trading the gold medal goalie." So Rask, the Maple Leafs' first-round pick in 2005, went to Boston for Raycroft, straight up, and Pogge stayed in Toronto.

Ferguson didn't consult Thommie Bergman, the Maple Leafs' head European scout, before pulling the trigger. He discovered Rask and would have fought to keep him; he knew the Savonlinna, Finland, native was the goalie of the future.

In his draft year Rask played for Ilves Tampere Juniors, posting a 17-3-4 record with a 1.86 goals-against average and .935 save percentage. While the trade played out in North America he stayed with Ilves in Finland's top league, before joining the American Hockey League's Providence Bruins in 2007.

Rask played in Providence for two seasons, with five cameo appearances for the big B's in Boston during that time. His first full NHL season came in 2009–10, after Rask took over for first-stringer Tim Thomas. Rask had a 22-12-5 record and led the NHL in both goals-against average (1.97) and save percentage (.931) before carrying the Bruins to Game 7 of the second round of the playoffs.

A year later, Thomas took the reins back and won both the 2011 Vezina and Conn Smythe Trophies as the Bruins lifted their first Stanley Cup since 1972. Rask earned a ring as the backup, and then assumed the number one role after the mercurial Thomas

Won bronze at the 2006 World Juniors and voted best goaltender

Won the Stanley Cup in 2011

Won bronze at the 2014 Olympics

Awarded the Vezina Trophy in 2014

Holds the highest career save percentage in NHL history (as of the start of 2017–18)

walked away from the team in 2012.

Playing on a one-year contract extension in 2012–13, Rask had a 19-10-5 record, 2.00 goals-against average and .929 save percentage. Facing Toronto in the first round of the 2013 playoffs, Boston came back from a 4–1 deficit in the third period of Game 7 and won in overtime. Rask won 14 playoff games with a league-high .940 save percentage and a 1.88 goals-against average, as the Bruins nearly upset the Chicago Blackhawks in the Stanley Cup Final.

On July 10, 2013, Rask was rewarded with an eight-year, $56 million contract. Rask repaid the Bruins' faith with 36 wins, a 2.04 goals-against average, a .930 save percentage and the Vezina Trophy in 2014. He also represented Finland at the 2014 Sochi Olympics; after sitting out the semifinal loss to bitter rival Sweden due to illness, he made 26 saves to shut out Team USA 5–0 and win the bronze medal.

In 2015 Rask achieved a different kind of immortality. A new breed of wasp found in Kenya by Robert Copeland, an entomologist who grew up in Massachusetts, was named *Thaumatodryinus tuukkaraski* in honor of Rask. Finland had funded the discovery, and a journal article about the bug said Rask's "glove hand is as tenacious as the raptorial fore tarsus of this dryinid species."

The tenacity earned Rask his first All-Star Game appearance in 2017 and a career-high 37 wins to lift the Bruins into a playoff position for the first time in three years.

If Rask's continued success more than a decade later isn't enough salt for Maple Leafs fans' wounds, it emerged later that Boston would've taken Pogge, who played all of seven NHL games in his career, and were considering releasing Raycroft anyway.

Raycroft lasted an uneven season and a half in Toronto and is now out of the game, while Rask, after 395 NHL games played at the end of the 2016–17 season, has the highest career save percentage in history at .923, .001 ahead of Hall of Famer Dominik Hasek.

That has to sting.

♠ 15

JACK EICHEL

ATLANTIC DIVISION | Sabres | Center

England, then in the East, then in the U.S. When he got to be 15, you knew he was one of the best his age in the whole world — a transcendent player."

The next step for Eichel was joining the U.S. National Development Team program in Ann Arbor, Michigan. It was a difficult move for the homebody who was only in his sophomore year of high school, but one that paid off for U.S. hockey and Eichel's career.

In 2013, at the age of 16, Eichel led the U.S. to a bronze medal at the World Under-17 Hockey Challenge and a silver medal at the Under-18 World Championship. In 2014 he was the Americans' youngest player at the World Junior Championship in Sweden, where he had five points in five games. Eichel was named captain for the 2015 World Juniors and finished his season at the World Championship, where he was the third-leading scorer on a bronze medal–winning team full of NHL players.

Eichel's collegiate hockey was played about 35 miles from home at Boston University. It was a brief but glorious time with the Terriers; he played one season, scoring 26 goals and 71 points in 40 games to lead the nation and became the second freshman ever to win the Hobey Baker Award as the best collegiate player in America.

According to veteran NHL scout Kevin Prendergast leading up to the 2015 entry draft, "It's not just his speed; it's his skill, his hockey sense. It doesn't even look like he's trying, but the puck comes to him. He makes things happen."

As the draft approached there was a made-for-TV rivalry between Eichel and Connor McDavid, the most sought after junior player since Sidney Crosby. The two had crossed paths in international competition a few times but didn't really know each other.

It was a win/win at the top of the draft, and the

In most entry drafts, Jack Eichel would've been the NHL's number one pick. The 6-foot-2, 196-pound center with vision, reach, patience and a cannon of a shot is the kind of player a team is built around. But 2015 was not most years.

Growing up in North Chelmsford, Massachusetts, Eichel wanted to play hockey at 4 years old but he couldn't sign up for the local league until he was 5. So, his parents, Bob and Anne, decided to register him in a league in New Hampshire instead of waiting. "Jack was one of the best players as soon he joined us," said Chris Masters, who coached Eichel with the Boston Junior Bruins. "But at 10 he started to separate from even the best kids. He became one of the top kids his age in Massachusetts, then in New

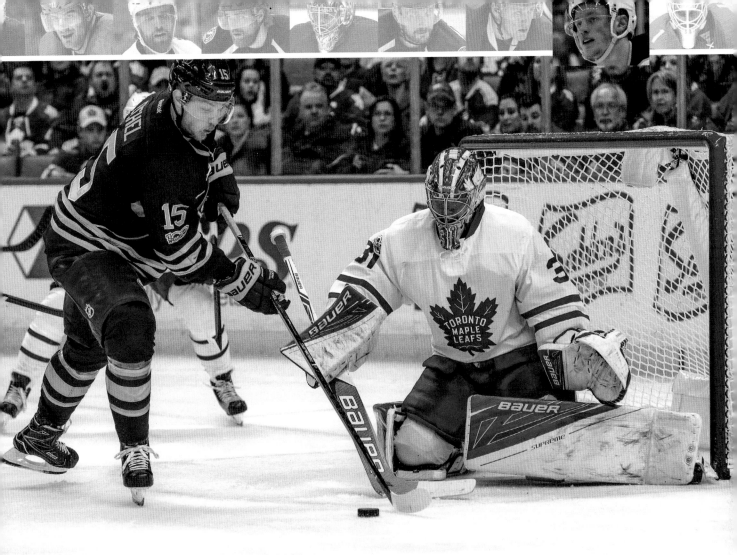

NHL changed its lottery so that teams didn't tank their season for one of the first two picks. "I can't remember a draft with two kids at the top like this since 2004, when [Alex] Ovechkin and [Evgeni] Malkin were 1-2," said Prendergast.

The Edmonton Oilers won the lottery and took McDavid, while the Buffalo Sabres happily chose Eichel second. He scored his first NHL goal in his first game; at 18 years and 345 days he was the youngest Sabre in history to score. Eichel led the Sabres with 24 goals in his rookie season, and he was second among all rookies in both goals and assists behind the Chicago Blackhawks' Artemi Panarin.

Prior to his second NHL season, Eichel was a member of the high-flying 23-and-under Team North America at the World Cup of Hockey. Full of confidence after an impressive 2-1 record versus the best in the world, Eichel suffered a serious ankle sprain in a scrimmage during Buffalo's training camp

and missed the first 21 games of the 2016–17 season. It was a blow for a team that was relying on the sophomore to lead them back to the playoffs for the first time since 2011. "I don't think of myself as a savior," said Eichel. "I just try to be an impact person and player in the locker room and on the ice every day. I try to bring my best as much as I can.

"More than anything you just assume a bigger role in terms of being a leader. You try to be better every day whether it's in practice or a game. I just try to make more of an impact on the guys every day. You can't use the rookie excuse anymore."

Captained the U.S. at the 2015 World Junior Championship

Won the 2015 Hobey Baker Award

Selected second overall in the 2015 NHL entry draft

Named to the 2016 NHL All-Rookie Team

86

NIKITA KUCHEROV

ATLANTIC DIVISION | Lightning | Right Wing

98

For a player knocking on the door of the Art Ross and Hart Trophies, Nikita Kucherov sure has a knack for making fleeting appearances on teams.

The Tampa Bay Lightning chose the Maykop, Russia, native in the second round of the 2011 entry draft, 58th overall, after he scored 58 points in 41 games with Krasnaya Armiya Moscow, the junior team of CSKA Moscow.

After being called up to the big club in the Kontinental Hockey League, Kucherov played only 26 games over two seasons. Seeing the success compatriot Nail Yakupov was having with the Ontario Hockey League's Sarnia Sting, he wanted out. CSKA granted Kucherov's release, and he signed with the Quebec

Remparts of the Quebec Major Junior Hockey League. He played all of six games for them.

With NHL players locked out in 2012 the Buffalo Sabres returned Mikhail Grigorenko to the Remparts. This put the team over its allotment of import players, so Kucherov was traded to the Rouyn-Noranda Huskies. Between the two teams he had 29 goals and 63 points in just 33 games. "Every time he's on the ice, he's dangerous," said former Remparts coach and Hall of Fame goalie Patrick Roy. "His IQ is really, really good. Off-the-charts. He sees the ice, he can sneak behind our Ds, he finds ways to get open. It's impressive."

Kucherov started 2013–14 with Tampa's American Hockey League affiliate. He had 13 goals and 24 points in 17 games, enough to convince the Lightning to call him up. Kucherov scored on the first shot of the first shift of his NHL career.

The rookie was still learning English and he spent the season soaking in the wisdom of Lightning elders like Martin St-Louis and Steven Stamkos. "I wasn't even saying anything," recalled Kucherov. "I was just looking around the room, watching guys, enjoying my time."

The 2014 playoffs brought more lessons for Kucherov. He was a healthy scratch for two games of a first round sweep by the Montreal Canadiens. The coaching staff didn't trust him defensively, but he watched and learned.

During the 2014–15 season Kucherov was put on a line with Ondrej Palat and Tyler Johnson. The "Triplets" had instant chemistry. Kucherov scored 29 goals while proving he'd taken the defensive lessons to heart with a plus-38 rating, which tied him for first in the NHL.

In the 2015 playoffs Kucherov had 10 goals, including two overtime winners, and 22 points in 26 games, as the Lightning lost to the Chicago

Blackhawks in the Stanley Cup Final. Tampa Bay reached the conference final again in 2016, with Kucherov scoring 11 goals in 17 games, but the Lightning didn't qualify for the 2017 postseason, despite his best efforts.

Kucherov had 27 goals and 50 points in the final 43 games to bring Tampa Bay within three points of a playoff spot. In one 16-game stretch he had 29 points, eight more than any player in the league during that span, and he scored 17 of his team's 45 goals.

Kucherov finished 2016–17 tied for second in the NHL in goals (40) and fifth in points (85), and Lightning defenseman Anton Stralman called him the team's best defensive player.

Ex-NHLer and current analyst Nick Kypreos thinks Kucherov's season put him among the league's elite: "We've got different looks now from McDavid, Crosby. But Kucherov is now in that conversation. You can tell he loves the big stage, and you can tell he's got ice in his veins. That's what you need to do to rise to the occasion."

Kucherov spoke out to the Russian media after the 2017 playoff push fell short: "Some guys over-stayed in team. They've got their money and stopped working. They knew there's no competition for their positions and the organization is not going to take someone else.

"When we played together and I made a pass, they even were not expecting this. That's why this season was hard (for) me despite good stats."

The interview was a bombshell in Tampa Bay, but Kucherov has earned the right as a leader of the Lightning and an established NHL star.

Won silver at the 2012 and bronze at the 2013 World Junior Championships

Tied for first in the NHL in plus-minus in 2014–15 (plus-38)

Tied for first in the NHL in power-play goals (17) in 2016–17

Played in the 2017 NHL All-Star Game

MORGAN RIELLY

ATLANTIC DIVISION | Maple Leafs | Defense

Growing up in West Vancouver, Morgan Rielly was one of those kids who could pick up any sport and excel immediately.

When he outgrew the local hockey system at 14 he moved to Wilcox, Saskatchewan, to play at hockey factory Notre Dame, a place he remembers fondly: "Just being in a dorm with three other guys who turn into your best friends and doing what you love — yeah, it was the best thing ever."

Rielly then went to Moose Jaw to play for the Warriors, who took him second overall in the Western Hockey League draft. In his second season he was ranked as high as second by NHL's Central Scouting, but he tore his ACL and played only 18 games.

The Toronto Maple Leafs were undeterred and took Rielly fifth overall in 2012. Then-general manager Brian Burke was attempting to craft a team in his truculent, belligerent image, but couldn't pass up the swift, creative defenseman.

After being drafted Rielly went back to Moose Jaw and scored 12 goals and 54 points, good for third and fifth, respectively, among WHL defenseman. He then finished the year playing 14 regular-season and five playoff games for the Toronto Marlies in the American Hockey League.

In 2013–14, at the age of 19, Rielly stuck with the Maple Leafs. He'd proven himself mature beyond his years. He played 73 games and was second among rookie defensemen in assists (25) and sixth in points (27). "He's got a personality where he's obviously dealt with a bunch of situations before so it's not like his first day at the office," said Randy Carlyle, Rielly's first coach with the Leafs.

Expectations were extremely high in Toronto for the 6-foot-1, 215-pound Rielly, and over the course of two more bleak years he was often the team's best player. He gave Leafs fans hope, a rare commodity in recent times in Canada's biggest market.

A regime change brought Brendan Shanahan and Lou Lamoriello to Toronto's front office and Mike Babcock behind the bench. Luck and savvy drafting gave the team William Nylander, Mitch Marner and Auston Matthews in 2016–17. Suddenly, at 22, the alternate captain became a veteran leader on one of the youngest, most exciting teams in the NHL.

With a high-performance offense developing, Babcock challenged Rielly to play more defensively and become one of the league's truly complete, two-way defensemen. After recovering from a high ankle sprain, Rielly finished strong and ranked fourth in the NHL at 30.7 shifts per game. "He's an elite player, he loves hockey, he's got a good engine," said

Babcock. "He comes with energy every day. I think he's one of the best young players in the world."

In March 2017 Rielly turned 23 and played his 300th NHL game, and a few weeks later the Maple Leafs clinched the first playoff berth of his career. Their prize was the first overall Washington Capitals, and the young Leafs took them to six games, five of which went to overtime.

In Game 4, Rielly was hit from behind and on the way down a skate blade cut his upper lip, adding to cuts across the bridge of his nose and under his eye. The Capitals scored on the play and Rielly was dripping blood. He shrugged it off after the loss: "Obviously it was a big play for them, they ended up scoring. That's just the way it goes."

He still can't grow a decent playoff beard, but Rielly has been through the growing pains and earned the scars. They're necessary reminders of the sacrifices and

commitment it takes to win in the NHL. But no one needs to remind the young leader. "I'm not one of those people who is able to float through life," said Rielly. "I definitely feel the stress, but I also accept that it's part of the job.

"You learn more from the tough times than you do from the good times and I think it's good to go through these things when you are young. It's a bit of an eye-opener and it's not all going to be easy."

Selected second overall in the 2009 WHL draft and fifth overall in the 2012 NHL entry draft

Won gold at the Ivan Hlinka Memorial Tournament in 2012

Won gold at the 2016 World Championship

Played for Team North America at the 2016 World Cup of Hockey

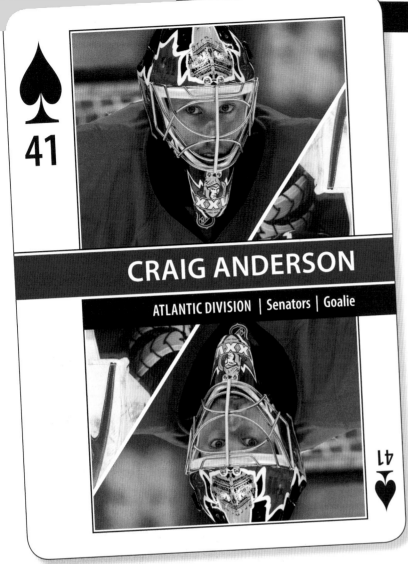

CRAIG ANDERSON

ATLANTIC DIVISION | Senators | Goalie

her husband to rejoin the team. In his first game back he had a 37-save shutout of the high-octane Oilers. When he accepted first star honors he had tears streaming down his face. For Anderson to even be in a position for such a storybook game is a triumph over adversity, in a hockey sense.

The Calgary Flames drafted Anderson in the third round, 77th overall, in 1999, but he didn't sign a contract. In 2000–01 his 30-19-9 record and 2.63 goals-against average with the Ontario Hockey League's Guelph Storm earned him the league's Goaltender of the Year Award.

Anderson reentered the entry draft in 2001, and the Chicago Blackhawks took the native of Park Ridge, Illinois, 73rd overall. He made his NHL debut on November 30, 2002, but didn't earn his first win until January 22, 2004, losing the first 13 decisions of his career.

It's not surprising, then, that Anderson only played 56 games for the Blackhawks over three seasons before he was put on waivers in January 2006. In the next 15 days he went from the Blackhawks to the Boston Bruins to the St. Louis Blues and back to the Blackhawks. The Florida Panthers acquired Anderson in 2006, and after 53 games in three years he signed as a free agent with the Colorado Avalanche in 2009. In his first season with the Avs he led the NHL in saves (2,047) and won 38 games.

The journey continued in February 2011 when the Avalanche traded Anderson to the Senators, and he immediately ingratiated himself with Ottawa fans by making 47 saves to shut out the provincial rival Toronto Maple Leafs in his first game. Ten games later Ottawa signed Anderson to a four-year, $13 million contract, and through the end of the season he had an 11-5-1 record, 2.05 goals-against average and .939 save percentage.

The world of sports, full of war metaphors and melodrama, has a way of elevating its own importance. But sometimes the bubble it exists in is punctured, reminding us it shouldn't be confused with real life struggle.

That perspective hit Craig Anderson during the 2016–17 season, when his wife, Nicholle, was diagnosed with cancer. It was another blow to the Senators family. Beloved assistant coach Roger Neilson lost his fight with it in 2003, Mark Reeds, another assistant coach, died in 2015, and senior hockey adviser Bryan Murray has Stage 4 cancer.

After Anderson took a leave of absence in October to be with his family, injuries left the Senators with two minor league goalies, so Nicholle encouraged

Since Anderson joined the Senators only five goalies have a better save percentage, and four have won the Vezina. "We know how good he is," said teammate Mark Stone, "but I think some people don't."

In the first two months of the 2016–17 season Anderson had a 1.49 goals-against average and a .952 save percentage before taking a lengthy leave of absence to take care of his wife and two sons. When he made his first start in 69 days on February 11 he shut out the New York Islanders 3–0.

Anderson and the Senators went on a magical run that nearly brought them to the Stanley Cup Final. Ottawa downed the Bruins and the New York Rangers on their way to facing the defending champion Pittsburgh Penguins in the Eastern Conference Final.

Anderson stole Game 6 with 45 saves in a 2–1 win, and stood on his head to keep Game 7 tied at the end of regulation. Ottawa had won six overtime games in the playoffs and seemed like a team of

destiny, but a Chris Kunitz knuckleball in double overtime ended the Senators' season. "Love," said Anderson when asked how he felt after the game. "The love for the guys in here. Right from the day I left the team to the day I came back. I wouldn't ask for better teammates than the guys this year."

And Nicholle tweeted: "A year you would think I would want to forget, but I couldn't be prouder of our team. Great year and memories that will last a lifetime."

A few days after the loss she was declared cancer-free. That's a trade her husband and the Senators would make any day.

Named the OHL's Goaltender of the Year in 2001	
Led the NHL in saves in 2009–10 (2,047)	
Led the NHL in save percentage in 2012–13 (.941)	
Awarded the Bill Masterton Memorial Trophy in 2017	

JAROMIR JAGR

ATLANTIC DIVISION | Panthers | Right Wing | 68

- Won the Stanley Cup twice (1991, 1992)
- Won the Art Ross Trophy five times (1995, 1998, 1999, 2000, 2001)
- Won gold at the 1998 Olympics
- Won the Hart Trophy in 1999
- Won the Ted Lindsay Award three times (1999, 2000, 2006)

ROBERTO LUONGO

ATLANTIC DIVISION | Panthers | Goalie | 1

- Won gold at the 2003 and 2004 World Championships
- Won gold at the 2004 World Cup of Hockey
- Won gold at the 2010 and 2014 Olympics
- Won the William Jennings Trophy in 2011
- Played in five NHL All-Star Games (2004, 2007, 2009, 2015, 2016)

lorida is a favorite destination of snowbirds and retirees, and though Jaromir Jagr and Roberto Luongo are on the back nine of their careers, neither is quite ready to fully commit to white shoes and early-bird dinners.

Luongo grew up in Saint-Leonard, Quebec, a few blocks from Martin Brodeur, the NHL's career leader in wins. At second overall in 1995, he was the highest drafted goalie in Quebec Major Junior Hockey League history, and two years later he earned the same distinction in the NHL when the New York Islanders took him fourth overall.

In a trade they've regretted for nearly two decades, the Islanders dealt Luongo to the Panthers in 2000, where he played for five seasons before he was traded to the Vancouver Canucks. The Panthers may also have had seller's remorse; in Luongo's first season with the Canucks in 2006–07 he won 47 games and was second in both Hart and Vezina Trophy voting.

Luongo was so popular in Vancouver he was voted captain of the Canucks, despite the fact it's against NHL rules. He had a "C" on his mask and in teammates' hearts, if not on his jersey.

Over more than seven seasons in Vancouver, Luongo won 252 games, including an NHL-best 38 in 2010–11, when the Canucks reached Game 7 of the Stanley Cup Final.

He was traded back to the Panthers in 2014, and by the conclusion of the 2016–17 season he had 966 games played, 453 wins, 73 shutouts and 26,264 saves in his career, all first among active goalies.

On the all-time list, Luongo enters the 2017–18 season third in games played and third in victories. Four more shutouts will put him past Tony Esposito and Ed Belfour into the top 10 in history.

In a win over the Buffalo Sabres on December 20, 2016, Luongo tied Terry Sawchuk with 447 career wins. In the same game Jagr equaled Mark Messier with 1,877 points for second in NHL history. Just another historic night for Luongo, the most interesting hockey player on Twitter (his Twitter handle is @strombone1), and Jagr, the most interesting hockey player in the world.

Jagr was born in 1972 in Kladno, Czechoslovakia (now the Czech Republic), and was playing junior hockey with kids up to 18 years old when he was 12. At 15 he became Zdenek Hrabe, a name he used to enter a senior international tournament because he wasn't old enough to participate.

Drafted fifth overall by the Pittsburgh Penguins in 1990 Jagr began his career as a sidekick to Mario Lemieux, with his mullet and arrogance flowing freely from under his helmet, and together they won the Stanley Cup in 1991 and 1992. Since then he has played for the Washington Capitals, New York Rangers, Philadelphia Flyers, Dallas Stars, Boston Bruins, New Jersey Devils and Panthers, as well as three seasons for Avangard Omsk in the Kontinental Hockey League from 2008–09 to 2010–11. He has won five Art Ross Trophies, three Lester B. Pearson (now Ted Lindsay) Awards, one Hart Trophy and one Olympic gold, most of them by the turn of the century when he was the best player in the world.

After passing Messier in points, Jagr's total of 1,914 at the start of 2017–18 is second in NHL history. If he plays 57 games in 2017–18 (he played all 82 in 2016–17) he'll pass Gordie Howe to become the NHL's all-time leader in games played.

At 45 Jagr is now the NHL's beloved uncle. The '90s are back in style so he grew the mullet back, and he still does 1,000 squats a day and drinks 10 cups of coffee, which is probably why he's been known to work out at 2 a.m.

Out of annoyance at the repeated question, Jagr once told reporters he'd retire at 60. That might've been an underestimation.

Jagr has chosen to play his 40s on a series of one-year contracts, and Luongo is locked up through 2020–21.

At the time of printing, it is yet to be determined where Jagr will play, but what's known for sure is neither Luongo nor Jagr will be joining younger players in alumni games or on the golf course anytime soon. Why would they when they're having this much fun?

METROPOLITAN DIVISION

FIRST STARS

50	**SIDNEY CROSBY**	Penguins	Center
52	**EVGENI MALKIN**	Penguins	Center
54	**ALEX OVECHKIN**	Capitals	Left Wing
56	**KRIS LETANG**	Penguins	Defense
58	**RYAN McDONAGH**	Rangers	Defense
60	**SERGEI BOBROVSKY**	Blue Jackets	Goalie

SECOND STARS

62	**NICKLAS BACKSTROM**	Capitals	Center
64	**JOHN TAVARES**	Islanders	Center
66	**TAYLOR HALL**	Devils	Left Wing
68	**SHAYNE GOSTISBEHERE**	Flyers	Defense
70	**SETH JONES**	Blue Jackets	Defense
72	**BRADEN HOLTBY**	Capitals	Goalie

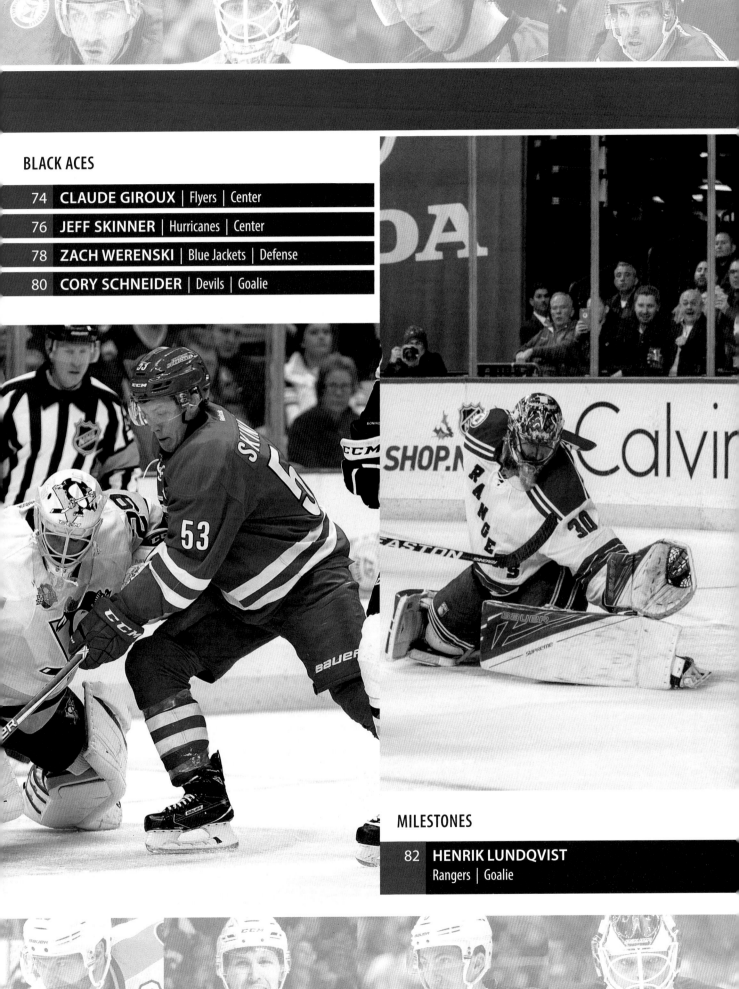

BLACK ACES

74	**CLAUDE GIROUX**	Flyers	Center
76	**JEFF SKINNER**	Hurricanes	Center
78	**ZACH WERENSKI**	Blue Jackets	Defense
80	**CORY SCHNEIDER**	Devils	Goalie

MILESTONES

| 82 | **HENRIK LUNDQVIST** |
| | Rangers | Goalie |

SIDNEY CROSBY

The mythology had already been established — from the dryer in the family basement in Cole Harbour that bore the brunt of his shooting practice to the Great One dubbing him "the Next Big Thing," to the Golden Goal — and in 2017 the legend of Sidney Crosby grew.

At the age of 7, Sid the Kid was "head and shoulders above everyone else his age," according to his hockey camp instructor and future Conn Smythe Trophy winner Brad Richards. "Kids usually peak. He never did."

When Crosby was 10, he had 280 points in 55 games, and he was 16 when Wayne Gretzky was asked if anyone could break his NHL records. "Yes, Sidney Crosby. He's the best player I've seen since Mario [Lemieux]."

Lemieux became Crosby's teammate, mentor, landlord and boss with the Pittsburgh Penguins, who drafted him first overall in 2005 after he led the Canadian Hockey League in scoring and won CHL Player of the Year two years in a row.

Entering the NHL the same year as the Washington Capitals' Alex Ovechkin, Crosby had 102 points — the youngest player in history with over 100 — but lost the 2006 Calder Trophy to Ovechkin, who had 52 goals and 106 points.

In their sophomore seasons, Crosby topped Ovechkin with 120 points to win both the 2007 Art Ross and Hart Trophies. He was the second-youngest MVP in NHL history, behind only Gretzky, and the youngest scoring champion in major professional sports history.

Named captain in 2007, the youngest in NHL history at the time, Crosby also became the youngest captain to lift the Stanley Cup in 2009.

With the 2010 Olympics on home soil, Canadians put their hopes and fears on Crosby's 22-year-old shoulders. He had a quiet tournament until the gold medal game when Crosby took a pass from Jarome Iginla and swept it between Ryan Miller's legs at 7:40 of overtime to give Canada a 3–2 victory over the U.S.

When facing each other internationally, Crosby has beaten Ovechkin on his way to gold in the 2005 World Juniors, the 2010 Olympics, the 2015 World Championship and the 2016 World Cup of Hockey. Though their teams didn't face each other, Crosby won his second Olympic gold on Ovechkin's turf at the 2014 Sochi Games.

Through fate and scheduling they remain tied together. On January 11, 2017, Ovechkin earned his 1,000th NHL point, against the Penguins, naturally. Five days later they played again and No. 87 — who was born on August 7, 1987 (8/7/87) — had a goal and three assists in an 8–7 win over the Capitals to tie him for 87th on the NHL's all-time scoring list.

A month later Crosby became the 11th youngest player with 1,000 career points, despite missing the equivalent of more than a full season due to serious concussion issues. Reaching it in 757 games he trailed only Gretzky, Lemieux, Bobby Orr and Mike Bossy on the career points-per-game list.

In some ways Crosby might be more a descendant of an NHL icon famous for his sharp elbows. Against the Buffalo Sabres in March 2017, Crosby had a twist on the Gordie Howe hat trick — he speared Ryan O'Reilly, scored arguably the goal of the season,

a one-handed backhand that he somehow managed to put top shelf, and then lost some teeth from a high stick to the mouth.

After winning the Stanley Cup in 2016 the Penguins repeated as champions in 2017. They became the first back-to-back winners in the 21st century, the first in the salary cap era and the first playing with a defense corps that hadn't received one Norris Trophy vote in their collective careers. With a lineup held together by hockey tape and hope, Crosby won his second straight Conn Smythe — the third player in history and first since Lemieux in 1991 and 1992.

Writing for *Sports Illustrated* prior to the season, Crosby said, "As if outrunning the downside of my career wasn't motivation enough, the new guys coming into the league will surely have my attention, too. These are the young and hungry guys. The guys that want to be where you are."

They have a mountain to climb. With three Stanley Cups before his 30th birthday Crosby isn't coming down from his perch atop the game anytime soon.

Won both the Art Ross and Hart Trophies in 2007 and 2014

Won the Ted Lindsay Award three times (2007, 2013, 2014)

Won the Stanley Cup three times (2009, 2016, 2017)

Won the Maurice Richard Trophy twice (2010, 2017)

Won the Conn Smythe Trophy twice (2016, 2017)

EVGENI MALKIN

Won the Calder Trophy in 2007

Won the Stanley Cup three times (2009, 2016, 2017)

Won the Conn Smythe Trophy in 2009

Won the Art Ross Trophy twice (2009, 2012)

Won the Hart Trophy and Ted Lindsay Award in 2012

At the 2017 All-Star weekend, the NHL named its top 100 players from its first 100 years. There were six active players on the list. Evgeni Malkin wasn't one of them.

These types of lists are hotly debated, but Geno was a glaring omission. There are few NHL players more decorated than Malkin, but one happens to be on his team, and that might explain the snub.

Malkin was born in Magnitogorsk, Russia, an iron and steel town on the Ural River. The resources gave the Metallurg hockey team its name, and he joined its system when he was 5 years old. At 17 Malkin was signed to Metallurg's senior team for the 2003–04 season. At the end of the year he was one of the greatest consolation prizes in NHL draft history, going second overall to the Pittsburgh Penguins, after the Washington Capitals took Alex Ovechkin.

Malkin played two more years in Magnitogorsk and had signed the richest contract in the Russian Super League, but he longed to be in America's Steel City. "He wanted to change everything," said his friend Andrei Zaitsev.

Like a Cold War defection, Malkin left the team during training camp in Helsinki and hid out until he could get his American visa. "This is pure sports terrorism," said Metallurg general manager Gennady Velichkin, who tried to sue the Penguins.

Sidney Crosby had already arrived in Pittsburgh as the top pick in 2005, and it soon became apparent that the Penguins had the 21st century version of Mario Lemieux and Jaromir Jagr.

Malkin made his Penguins debut in 2006–07 and didn't disappoint. He set a modern-day record by scoring in each of his first six games. The only other player to do that was Joe Malone of the Montreal Canadiens in 1917–18. Malkin finished the year with 33 goals, 85 points and the Calder Trophy.

The ascendant Penguins lost the 2008 Stanley Cup Final to the Detroit Red Wings, after Malkin had 106 regular season points. A year later he led the

league in scoring with 113 points, and the Penguins beat the Red Wings in a rematch to win the Stanley Cup. With 14 goals and 36 points in 24 games, Malkin became the second-youngest player in history to win the Conn Smythe Trophy.

Over his first four seasons Malkin was one of only three players to average more than a point a game each year, Crosby and Ovechkin being the other two. In 2011 he was averaging just under a point a game when he tore his ACL and MCL, which ended his season and his streak. For the first time his body had let him down.

Malkin returned in 2011–12 with a chip on his shoulder and the team on his back. With Crosby suffering from post-concussion syndrome, Malkin had a career-high 50 goals and 109 points to win his second Art Ross. He also won the Hart Trophy and the Ted Lindsay Award.

"With Sid out, teams are paying more attention to him," said teammate Kris Letang. "They're playing him harder. And he likes that."

At 6-foot-3 and 195 pounds, Malkin can do it with power and finesse, a rare combination that's reminiscent of Lemieux. Only Crosby and Peter Forsberg have a higher points-per-game average then Malkin over the past 20 years. The only active players with more goals per game are Ovechkin, Steven Stamkos and Crosby, by a few percentage points. "In sheer skill level Geno probably has to be rated higher [than Crosby]," said former Pittsburgh coach Dan Bylsma. "There's magic there, a little bit different than what Sid has."

Together Malkin and Crosby won their second Stanley Cup in 2016, and then went past Lemieux and Jagr with a third in 2017. Malkin led all scorers with 28 points in the playoffs that season.

While the Penguins celebrated, general manager Jim Rutherford mused about the 100 Greatest Players list of a few months earlier. "Maybe we can re-vote and see if Malkin is in the top 100 now."

ALEX OVECHKIN

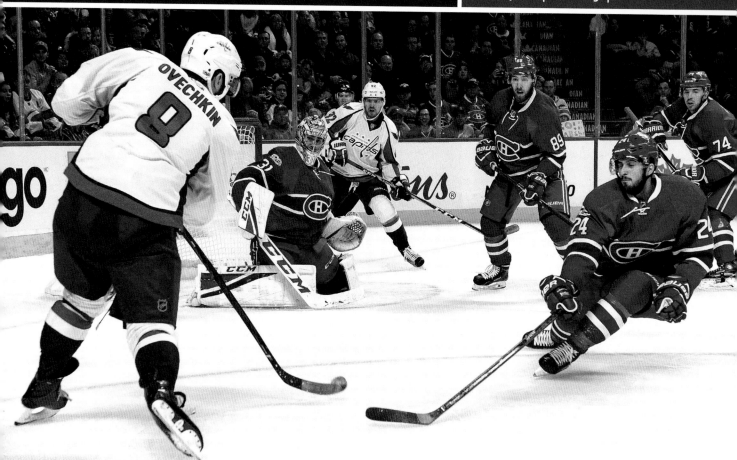

One of hockey's enduring clichés is that it's a game of inches. For Alex Ovechkin the perception of his career might come down to roughly the width of the shaft on a goalie stick.

Down 1–0 in Game 7 of the second round in the 2017 playoffs, the captain of the Presidents' Trophy–winning Washington Capitals was alone in the slot for a one-timer that was headed for the top corner and a tie, until the smallest part of Marc-Andre Fleury's goalie equipment intervened.

Maybe the Capitals wouldn't have beaten the Pittsburgh Penguins anyway, but it fed into the narrative that Ovechkin disappears in the biggest games.

Ovechkin was selected first overall in 2004, and Sidney Crosby was the top pick in 2005 by the Penguins. After the 2004–05 lockout they made their NHL debuts in 2005–06, and though they have contrasting personalities and styles, they've been compared ever since.

In his first NHL game Ovechkin scored twice and hit an opponent so hard that a partition broke. "Within a week or so we knew that we had a real special human being here," said Glen Hanlon, Ovechkin's first NHL coach.

Later in the season he showed the rest of the world, and the Great One, who was coaching the Phoenix Coyotes at the time. Facing the Coyotes on January 16, 2006, Ovechkin was knocked down and sliding on his back as he drove to the net, but somehow hooked the puck past a stunned Brian Boucher in goal. It was the highlight of the decade, now simply called "The Goal," and it's still Ovechkin's favorite. "My dream was come true: I play in the NHL, I did that kind of special goal and [Wayne] Gretzky was there, as well," he said.

"You could really feel the announcement of the superstar," according to then-teammate Brooks Laich. "You could feel it in the building as clear as day."

A decade later, on January 10, 2016, Ovechkin became the fifth-fastest player to reach 500 goals.

The 2015–16 season was his seventh with at least 50 goals, which made him just the third player in NHL history with seven or more, joining Gretzky and Mike Bossy, who each did it nine times in a far more freewheeling and offensive era.

A year and a day after his 500th goal, Ovechkin scored 35 seconds into a game against the Penguins to earn his 1,000th point in his 880th game. He is the second-fastest active player to reach the milestone, after Jaromir Jagr.

Crosby reached 1,000 points a month after Ovechkin, and they're one-two in goals and points since 2005–06, when they entered the league. At the end of the 2016–17 season Ovechkin's 558 goals were 176 ahead of Crosby's, and his 1,035 points were eight more.

Ovechkin beat out Crosby for the 2006 Calder Trophy and has since won the Hart Trophy and Ted Lindsay Award three times each, the Maurice Richard Trophy six times and the Art Ross Trophy once, but he's said that he would "trade them all for one Stanley Cup."

The Penguins ended that dream in 2016 and 2017 on their way to consecutive titles — both times after the Capitals finished first overall — and each of Crosby's three Stanley Cups went through Washington in the second round.

Only five players have had more goals than Ovechkin and never won the Stanley Cup, and Ovechkin and Marcel Dionne (684 goals) are the two highest-scoring players never to reach a conference final.

But the losses won't break Alexander the Gr8. The 6-foot-3, 239-pound Muscovite wrecking ball is tough. When Ovie was 10, his older brother and idol Sergei died after a car accident, and growing up in a post-communist Russia most of his friends were "getting high and getting dead," according to Ovechkin. He attended an authoritarian school but left early to escape into hockey. "You dive into sport with your head and arms and legs, and there's no time for anything else," he explained. "There's no other career."

For Ovechkin, this generation's purest and most exciting goal-scorer, it's a Hall of Fame career. Even if the Great Hall in Toronto is the closest he ever gets to the Stanley Cup.

Won the Hart Trophy three times (2008, 2009, 2013)

Won the Ted Lindsay Award three times (2008, 2009, 2010)

Won the Art Ross Trophy in 2008

Won the Maurice Richard Trophy six times (2008, 2009, 2013, 2014, 2015, 2016)

Won gold at the 2008, 2012 and 2014 World Championships

KRIS LETANG

METROPOLITAN DIVISION

Penguins | Defense | 58

- Won gold at the 2006 and 2007 World Junior Championships
- Named the QMJHL's Defenseman of the Year in 2007
- Won the Stanley Cup three times (2009, 2016, 2017)
- Played in three NHL All-Star Games (2011, 2012, 2016)

On the morning of January 29, 2014, Kris Letang woke up dizzy and disoriented. Determined to go on the Pittsburgh Penguins' mother-son road trip, he ignored the symptoms and got on the plane.

Team doctor Dharmesh Vyas didn't let Letang play that night in Los Angeles, and arranged for an MRI the next day when the Penguins were in Arizona. Letang, at 26, had suffered a stroke. It was the result of an undiagnosed heart defect that's common in babies but usually repairs itself. "The whole time, he maintained a really strong perspective on what was going on, but also [remained] extremely optimistic that he was going to continue to play," said Vyas.

That perspective was hard earned, because the specter of an athletic career cut short doesn't compare to what Letang had already endured.

In 2003 the Quebec Major Junior Hockey League's Val-d'Or Foreurs drafted Luc Bourdon third over-all and Letang 27th. During the 2004–05 season, Bourdon and Letang each had 13 goals and 19 assists in 70 games, and together they won gold medals with Team Canada at the 2006 and 2007 World Juniors.

Bourdon was drafted 10th overall by the Vancouver Canucks in 2005, while the Penguins took Letang 62nd overall. They remained close as their NHL careers took off. After winning the Emile Bouchard Trophy as the QMJHL's Defenseman of the Year in 2007, Letang reached the Stanley Cup Final in his first full season with the Penguins. On May 29, 2008, as Pittsburgh was battling Detroit for the Cup, Bourdon died in a motorcycle crash in his native New Brunswick at the age of 21.

One year later, after the Penguins defeated the Red Wings in a Stanley Cup rematch, Letang got a tattoo dedicated to Bourdon and his grandmother.

"Every time I step on the ice he's in my thoughts." said Letang. "He was a guy that embraced every day of hockey. Every night I think about him before games, making sure I'm ready and all the things he taught me."

With that inspiration, Letang established himself as a young star and the anchor of the Penguins defense — a smooth-skating, puck-moving defenseman who eats minutes and can be deployed in any situation. "He's a guy I tell my kid to watch all the time," said Hall of Fame defenseman and former Penguin Paul Coffey in 2011. "He's strong, smart, tough. He can shoot the puck. He doesn't look big, but he's strong on his feet and he's very heads-up."

Letang was a Norris Trophy finalist after 38 points in 35 games in the lockout-shortened 2012–13 season, but between 2011 and 2015 he missed 102 games due to ailments, including multiple concussions. When Letang has been healthy he's averaged 0.64 points per game, which is third among defensemen with at least 500 games played since he entered the league. "I honestly think Kris doesn't get the recognition in the hockey world that he deserves," said Penguins coach Mike Sullivan. "[He's] one of most elite defensemen that this league has."

Back to full strength in 2015–16, Letang averaged almost 27 minutes a game and was third among defenseman with 67 points. In the postseason he averaged just under 29 minutes and had 15 points in 23 games, including the Stanley Cup–winning goal in Game 6 against the San Jose Sharks.

The Penguins repeated as champions in 2017, and despite not playing in the postseason, Letang got his name on the Cup for the third time. He played the minimum 41 regular season games to be eligible before neck surgery to repair a herniated disc ended his season, and acted as a de facto assistant coach, imparting veteran wisdom and offering inspiration. "Just having him there is a big boost," said teammate Bryan Rust. "We know how bad he wants to be out there and how much he means to this team and this organization. Just knowing he wishes so bad to be out there kind of fuels us that much more."

RYAN McDONAGH

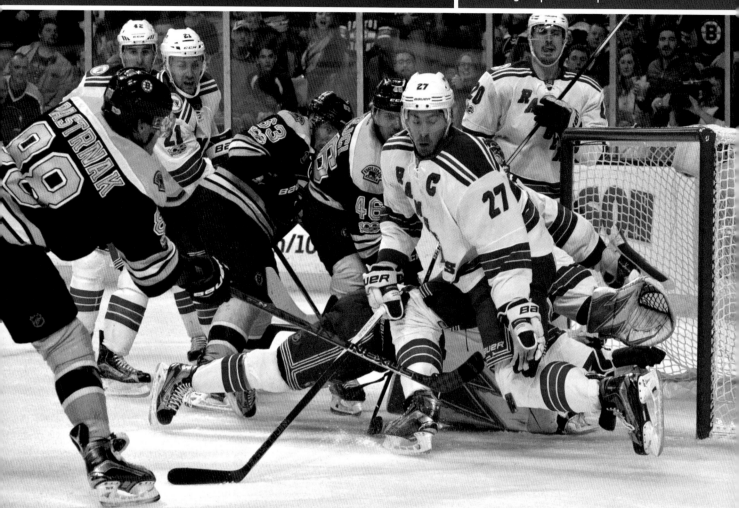

Until 2017 Ryan McDonagh lived in a loft a few floors below Taylor Swift in Manhattan. He's also a few levels down on the celebrity scale in New York City, even while leading the Rangers at Madison Square Garden, a.k.a. the World's Most Famous Arena.

McDonagh is not exactly the Mark Messier type. The captain and lone representative for the Rangers at the 2016 and 2017 All-Star Games retains his Midwestern modesty and reserve after years in New York.

McDonagh is married to his high school sweetheart, Kaylee, whom he met at Cretin-Derham Hall in St. Paul, Minnesota. As a junior in 2006 he led Cretin-Derham to its first state championship, and in his senior year he had 14 goals and 40 points in 26 games and was named Minnesota's Mr. Hockey.

The summer after graduating high school McDonagh was drafted 12th overall by the Montreal Canadiens. He'd never dress for them, however, a decision they'd come to rue.

In 2009, after two seasons at the University of Wisconsin, McDonagh was traded to the Rangers in an eight-player deal that included Scott Gomez going back to Montreal. Gomez flopped in Montreal, even going 369 days between goals, while New York knew it had a future star. "In my time at the [draft] combine, he's been the single most impressive guy ever," said Gordie Clark, Rangers director of player personnel.

Back in Wisconsin for his junior year McDonagh helped the Badgers reach the 2010 NCAA Frozen Four championship game, where they lost to Boston College. At that point he believed he'd accomplished all he could in college. "I just felt I learned a ton in my three years there and developed physically," McDonagh said. "I felt confident and ready, and excited for a new challenge."

McDonagh signed an entry-level contract with the Rangers in 2010, and after his first NHL training camp was sent to the Connecticut Whale in the American Hockey League. He played 38 games in the AHL before making his NHL debut on January 7, 2011.

In 2011–12 McDonagh became an NHL regular — averaging 24:44 over 82 games — and in 2014 he took his place among the game's elite. He was a stalwart on the Team USA blue line at the Sochi Olympics, and in the playoffs he got a little revenge against the team that traded him. In the first game of the 2014 Eastern Conference Final against the Canadiens, McDonagh had a goal and three assists in a 7–2 victory. He was the first Rangers defenseman with four points in a playoff game since Brian Leetch in the 1994 Stanley Cup Final.

McDonagh isn't one to gloat though. Asked if he took pleasure in teaching Montreal a lesson he replied, "No, just the satisfaction of winning the first game of the series."

Whether there was extra incentive or not, McDonagh set a team record among defensemen with eight assists in the series, and he finished the 2014 postseason with four goals and 17 points in 25 games. Three weeks after the Rangers lost the 2014 Stanley Cup Final to the Los Angeles Kings, McDonagh was named the 27th captain in team history, and the fourth youngest.

"We were shocked when he got the captaincy because he's not an out-front person," said McDonagh's father, Sean. "He's a stand-in-the-back-of-the-room guy that does his job and moves on."

Since McDonagh was named captain, the Rangers have played in six playoff series in three seasons, including a second-round loss to the Ottawa Senators

in 2017. In the first three games of the series, Erik Karlsson, the Senators' two-time Norris Trophy winner, played 90:08 minutes, had a goal, an assist, six blocked shots and three hits. Playing in one of the league's smallest markets, the flashy Swede also captured all the attention and headlines.

With little fanfare the steady McDonagh played 89:36, had a goal, an assist, 12 blocked shots and 17 hits, including 11 in a Game 2 double-overtime loss. "[McDonagh] is one of the best defensemen in the league," according to teammate Jimmy Vesey. "Karlsson is obviously world-class offensively, but Ryan, just with his skating ability and how strong he is, he's one of the best defenders I've seen."

Named Mr. Hockey in the state of Minnesota in 2007	
Selected to the Western Collegiate Hockey Association All-Rookie team in 2008	
Voted MVP and named captain of the New York Rangers in 2014	
Played in two NHL All-Star Games (2016, 2017)	

SERGEI BOBROVSKY

Won the Vezina Trophy twice (2013, 2017)

Led the NHL in goals-against average (2.06) and save percentage (.931) in 2016–17

Played in two NHL All-Star Games (2015, 2017)

Won gold at the 2014 World Championship

The Columbus Blue Jackets were the NHL's biggest surprise in 2016–17, finishing the season fourth overall, up from 27th the year before.

Much of the credit goes to goalie Sergei Bobrovsky, "the backbone of our team," according to coach John Tortorella. Having won his first Vezina Trophy in 2013, Bobrovsky had fallen on hard times in recent years, plagued by groin injuries that robbed him of his swagger. "He openly said last year he lost his confidence," said Blue Jackets GM Jarmo Kekalainen. "If there's one position where lost confidence can be seen very easily, it is goaltending."

Bobrovsky is a gym rat, not always a common trait among the goalie fraternity, but the extra weight that he carried in muscle was working against him. So prior to the 2016–17 season he changed his diet and workout regime and dropped about 15 pounds.

"You look at his body last year and the body composition, and all his body fats and all that, you'd say it was impossible," said Kekalainen. "But he did it. He basically sculpted his body into a different form in the off-season ... That just tells you about his dedication and how serious he is about his professionalism and how he approaches every day."

Having grown up in Siberia, Bobrovsky comes by his work ethic honestly. His father was a coal miner, and his mother worked on the line at a steel factory.

Undrafted in 2006, Bobrovsky spent three seasons with his hometown Metallurg Novokuznetsk in the Kontinental Hockey League before the Philadelphia Flyers offered him a contract in 2010. He made his NHL debut in Philly's first game of 2010–11, becoming the youngest goalie in Flyers history to start a season. He spoke very little English and kept his instructions to the players around him to just a few words. "It could be beneficial," said Jeff Reese, Bobrovsky's goalie coach at the time. "He's just going out and playing. He's simplifying things, and to me [his not speaking English] is simplifying. Maybe he doesn't quite understand, especially in Philly, with the goal-

tending and everything, that there's a lot of pressure."

The city and franchise do have a way of chewing up and spitting out goaltenders, and Bobrovsky only lasted two years in the City of Brotherly Love before being traded to the Blue Jackets in 2012.

It paid immediate dividends in Ohio. Bobrovsky won the Vezina in the lockout-shortened 2012–13 season and finished fifth in Hart Trophy voting.

In 2014 Bobrovsky returned home to represent Russia at the Sochi Olympics. It was a disappointing showing for the host country, but Bobrovsky was third in the tournament in goals-against average (1.15) and save percentage (.952).

There was redemption for Russia at the 2014 World Championship, as Bobrovsky led the team to gold and the tournament in goals-against average (1.13) and save percentage (.950).

The following seasons weren't as kind to Bobrovsky, and the low point was 2015–16. He only played 37 games because of injuries, and his 2.75 goals-against

average and .908 save percentage were the second-worst of his career.

But newly lean and flexible, Bobrovsky began the 2016–17 season by shutting out Finland and sending Russia to the semifinals of the World Cup of Hockey. He stopped 91 of 96 shots in the tournament and stood on his head in the semis against eventual champion Canada, with 42 saves, but couldn't propel his team in the final.

"Bob" had been put back together again, in mind and body, and his 2.06 goals-against average and .931 save percentage in 2016–17 both led the NHL. He had a career-high 41 wins and won the Vezina for the second time. "I feel very good," said Bobrovsky during the World Cup. "Yeah, I had some tough times obviously, but I feel great right now and I feel ready mentally and physically. It helps you because you believe in your body. You know you can rely on your body and everything works in the proper way.

"It's all about processes. You move on every day."

NICKLAS BACKSTROM

METROPOLITAN DIVISION

Capitals | Center | 19

If you research Nicklas Backstrom's accomplishments you might think he played in the 2009 NHL All-Star Game. He didn't, that was Niklas (not Nicklas), the Finnish goalie who spent 10 years in the NHL. And don't confuse him with the other Niklas Backstrom, who is Swedish like Nicklas but a mixed martial arts fighter.

It's typical of the hockey-playing Swedish Backstrom to be lost in the shuffle, and frankly he doesn't care. "Nick's not that person that seeks attention or wants to be that way," said Henrik Zetterberg, who's played with Backstrom on Team Sweden. "He doesn't want to stand out."

It's fitting, then, that Alex Ovechkin took the stage to announce the Washington Capitals had selected Backstrom fourth overall at the 2006 draft. While Backstrom would be at center and Ovechkin on the wing, there's a strong gravitational pull around Ovie, which means everything orbits around him in Washington.

Backstrom spent the season after the draft playing for Brynas IF in his hometown of Gavle, the same team his father was on for 10 seasons. He was named the Swedish Elite League's Rookie of the Year in 2006, and he became the youngest player to represent Sweden at the 2006 World Championship, where he won a gold. "Even when he was young, he was strong-minded," recalled Leif Boork, Backstrom's coach at Brynas. "My first impression was that this guy, he's the new Peter Forsberg."

In 2007–08, his first season with the Capitals, Backstrom set a franchise rookie record with 55 assists. He was the first rookie in NHL history with consecutive games of at least four assists and finished second to Patrick Kane in Calder Trophy voting. In the playoffs he scored in four straight games in a first round loss, a sign of things to come.

Backstrom, who led the NHL in assists with 60 in 2014–15, has since become the first player in franchise history with 500 career assists. The milestone came on January 7, 2017, on a T.J. Oshie goal against the Ottawa Senators. Four days later Backstrom set up Ovechkin for the Russian sniper's 1,000th career point. Over the decade they've played together, Backstrom has assisted on roughly 45 percent of Ovechkin's goals.

At the end of the 2016–17 season Backstrom had 540 assists and 728 points in 734 games. Only Joe Thornton and Henrik Sedin had more assists in that time, and just five players had more points. The players ahead of him combined for eight Hart Trophies and 29 All-Star Game appearances.

Backstrom, on the other hand, wasn't named to his first All-Star Game until 2016, his ninth season. He had already booked a family vacation but cancelled it to attend. "It's funny," said Washington coach Barry Trotz. "He's going, 'I've never been. What should I expect?' I'm looking at him, and I'm going, 'You should have been there like 10 times already.'"

When asked about the lack of recognition, Backstrom said, "I don't really care about that stuff. There's a little bit of Swedish culture, I think, to put your team in front of yourself."

It's a positive attitude to have when the best Backstrom has ever finished for an individual award is 10th in Selke Trophy voting.

Backstrom wasn't selected to play in the 2017 All-Star Game, despite finishing the 2016–17 season second to Connor McDavid with 63 assists and fourth overall with 86 points, 17 more than Ovechkin, who played in his eighth All-Star Game.

The fact that the Capitals have failed to live up to expectations and consecutive Presidents' Trophies in the playoffs, as they did in 2016 and 2017, may be a contributing factor. Stars are born in the bright lights of the playoffs, but blending in can be a blessing, too. Backstrom didn't bear the brunt of criticism for the Capitals failures, but with 24 points in 25 games over those two playoffs it would've been unwarranted.

So maybe his persona and staying on the periphery is Backstrom's masterstroke.

"When he's said and done and you probably look at his numbers, you're going to go those might be the quietest Hall of Fame numbers that we've ever seen," according to Trotz. "He's going to have some terrific numbers when he's done."

Named the Swedish Elite League's Rookie of the Year in 2006

Won gold at the 2006 and 2017 World Championships

Won silver at the 2014 Olympics

Played in the 2016 NHL All-Star Game

JOHN TAVARES

John Tavares is the National Lacrosse League's all-time leading scorer; his nephew John Tavares, captain of the New York Islanders, is a pretty decent athlete himself.

The younger John was so talented that he became the first player to be granted Exceptional Player Status by the Ontario Hockey League, when he was just 14. The Mississauga, Ontario, native was then selected first overall in the 2005 OHL draft by the Oshawa Generals.

In his rookie year Tavares had 45 goals and 77 points to win both the OHL and Canadian Hockey League Rookie of the Year awards. In his second year he had 72 goals and 134 points, breaking Wayne Gretzky's record for goals by a 16-year-old and taking home the OHL's Most Outstanding Player and CHL Player of the Year awards.

Tavares finished his junior career with the London Knights. He led the OHL with 58 goals and 104 points in his final season and won gold and MVP honors at the 2009 World Junior Championship.

The Islanders took Tavares first overall in 2009, and in 2011–12 he had 81 points in 82 games, becoming the fourth under-21 player in franchise history to score at least 73 points. The other three — Mike Bossy, Bryan Trottier and Denis Potvin — are all Hall of Famers. It was also the first time an Islander had 70 points or more in a season since Alexei Yashin in 2001–02 and 50 assists since Pierre Turgeon in 1993–94. The Islanders and their long-suffering fans were justifiably excited.

In 2013 Tavares was named the 14th captain in team history. He was a no-brainer for Team Canada at the 2014 Sochi Olympics; however, in a game against Latvia he tore ligaments in his left knee. He won gold while on the injured reserve but was lost for the rest of the NHL season.

After a full recovery prior to 2014–15, Tavares had his best season to date, finishing second in the NHL with 86 points and being named a Hart Trophy finalist.

- Named the OHL's Most Outstanding Player and CHL Player of the Year in 2007
- Won the 2009 World Junior Championship and named tournament MVP
- Played in four NHL All-Star Games (2012, 2015, 2016, 2017)
- Won gold at the 2014 Olympics
- Won the World Cup of Hockey in 2016

Tavares spread more joy to Isles fans in the 2016 playoffs. He had the tying goal in the last minute of Game 6 against the Florida Panthers and scored in double overtime to clinch the series. It was the first time the Islanders had reached the second round since 1993, and Tavares was the first player in their illustrious playoff history to score the tying goal in the final minute of regulation and the winner in overtime.

The Islanders regressed in 2016–17, but Tavares had one of the NHL's highlights of the year in a December game against the St. Louis Blues. With his arm being held by Jay Bouwmeester he passed his stick to himself behind his back to free it, stickhandled away from three Blues and roofed the puck. This moment was a display of the creativity and determination that have made Tavares one of the NHL's best.

Only four players have scored more goals than Tavares since he was drafted — Alex Ovechkin, Steven Stamkos, Corey Perry and Sidney Crosby —

and when his contract expires in 2018 he'll be one of the most sought after free agents in NHL history. In addition to possibly losing their best player, the Islanders are also facing eviction from the Barclays Center in Brooklyn, where they moved in 2015 after 43 years at the Nassau Coliseum.

Fans have endured a lot of dysfunction since the Islanders' glory days in the early 1980s, and losing Tavares could be a death-blow. But he's as honest as he is exceptional and he's given no indication he's looking for a divorce. "They drafted me there, gave me a great opportunity to play this game that I love and fulfill my dream. They've put a lot of high expectations into me and I don't take that lightly," said Tavares. "I'd like to see that through and obviously lift the Stanley Cup there."

If he's anything like his uncle, who retired after 24 years with the NLL's Buffalo Bandits, the Islanders faithful have years of loyal leadership from John Tavares ahead of them. Wherever they may play.

TAYLOR HALL

K im Strba and Steve Hall were pondering a move back to Ontario from Calgary but couldn't decide where to settle. Kim had family in Toronto, Windsor and Kirkland Lake, Australian-born Steve had grown up in London and they'd met at the University of Guelph.

So they chose Kingston. "There was a method to the madness," according to Steve. They didn't want to live too close to relatives so they came up with a "100 mile rule" when relocating.

Steve was a former receiver in the Canadian Football League, and he'd moved his family to Calgary while he was training with the national bob-sled team. Their 13-year-old son Taylor, however, was all about hockey. "I had come through this way to

play football in Ottawa" said Steve. "I knew it was on water and it was a little farther north, so if you had to build a rink you could. Those things have to be taken into consideration when you have a hockey player."

Taylor Hall was just entering high school when they moved, and the transition wasn't easy. His first season with the Greater Kingston Predators was mediocre as he and his family settled into their new surroundings, but things clicked in his second season with the Predators. The midget team went 27-4 in the regular season and earned a berth in the OHL Cup, a showcase for clubs from Canada and the United States. "The difference with him was that he loved it," said Hall's midget coach Mike Fiset. "You can't teach that. He was always one of the first on and the last off. When that's one of your better players, that's a great example for your team."

The Windsor Spitfires took notice and picked Hall second overall in the 2007 Ontario Hockey League draft. He was named Canadian Hockey League Rookie of the Year in 2008, and in 2009 he won the Wayne Gretzky 99 Award as OHL playoff MVP and the Stafford Smythe Trophy as tournament MVP after leading the Spitfires to the Memorial Cup championship.

The following season was dominated by the Taylor/Tyler debate over who would go first overall in the 2010 NHL entry draft. Fittingly, Hall and Tyler Seguin tied for the OHL scoring title, but Windsor won its second straight Memorial Cup and Hall became the first player in history to win tournament MVP honors in consecutive seasons.

The rebuilding Edmonton Oilers selected Hall first overall, and he went on to break a couple of Wayne Gretzky's Oiler records. Hall recorded the fastest hat trick from the start of a game on March 30, 2013, scoring three in the first 7:53 of a 4–0 win over the Vancouver Canucks, which bettered Gretzky's 12:38 in 1985–86. The second came on October 17, 2013, when Hall scored twice in eight seconds in a 3–2 loss to the New York Islanders, which topped Gretzky for the quickest two goals in team history by one second.

The best player on a struggling team, Hall emerged as a leader of the youth movement in Edmonton. He had 328 points in 381 games in six seasons, leading the team in scoring three times and finishing among the NHL's top 10 scorers twice.

The Oilers had been stockpiling offensive talent with high draft picks, including Connor McDavid, and needed help on defense, but it still came as a shock when they made a deal with the Devils.

Edmonton sent Hall to New Jersey in a rare 1-for-1 trade for defenseman Adam Larsson in the summer of 2016.

Edmonton general manager Peter Chiarelli, who has the distinction of trading both Taylor and Tyler, the latter when he was managing the Boston Bruins, hadn't included Hall among the people he sat down with at the end of the 2015–16 season. "He didn't say anything like that to me so that's why I was really caught off guard when it happened," said Hall, who admitted harboring resentment toward the organization, while also keeping tabs on Edmonton early in 2016–17. "If they win the Cup, I'll be choked. I think like the first 15 or 20 games they played this year, every game I'd be on my phone waiting to see how they did. Now I don't really care as much."

Edmonton made a long-awaited return to the playoffs in 2017 while New Jersey missed out, but if history is any indication the magic will begin in Hall's second season after moving east from Alberta.

Named CHL Rookie of the Year in 2008

Won back-to-back Memorial Cups in 2009 and 2010 and named MVP for both

Selected first overall at the 2010 NHL entry draft

Played in two NHL All-Star Games (2016, 2017)

SHAYNE GOSTISBEHERE

METROPOLITAN DIVISION

Flyers | Defense | 53

Say what you will about commissioner Gary Bettman's Great Southern Experiment in terms of fan engagement and franchise solvency, but it is starting to produce high-end talent from some unlikely places.

Shayne Gostisbehere was born in Pembroke Pines, Florida, in 1993, the same year the Florida Panthers came into the NHL. His father, Regis, had moved there from France to play jai alai (a sport in which a ball is bounced off a walled court using a curved handheld device), where he met his French-Canadian bride-to-be, Christine, working at a jai alai court.

Shayne's sister Felicia took figure skating lessons at the Panthers' training facility in Coral Springs, and he would tag along. He eventually stuck around the rink as a member of the Junior Panthers. His dad knew little about the game, so his maternal grandfather, Denis, helped out. "I bought him a helmet, got him into a league and coached him for years before [former Panther] Ray Sheppard took over," said Denis. "He was always the smallest kid on the team, but I told him there are two things he has to remember: 'Let your stick and skates do the talking and no one will turn you down.'"

With his grandfather's wise words in mind, Gostisbehere left Florida to play hockey at South Kent School in Connecticut for his final two years of high school. He had 36 points in 24 games as a senior but went undrafted in 2011. Philadelphia took a flyer on Ghost in the 2012 draft, choosing him in the third round, 78th overall, after his first season at Union College in Schenectady, New York.

The Flyer scouts earned their pay. Gostisbehere won a gold medal with Team USA at the 2013 World Junior Championship, and in 2014 he was named Frozen Four MVP as Union won its first national championship. In the title game at Philadelphia's Wells Fargo Center he had a goal, two assists and was plus-7 in a 7–4 win over the University of Minnesota.

Flyer fans would have to wait for him to light up the rink again, however. After five games with the

Won gold at the 2013 World Junior Championship

Won the NCAA championship and named Frozen Four MVP in 2014

Played in the 2016 NHL All-Star Game

Set the NHL record for longest point streak by a rookie defenseman (15 games)

Holds the NHL rookie record with four overtime goals in a season

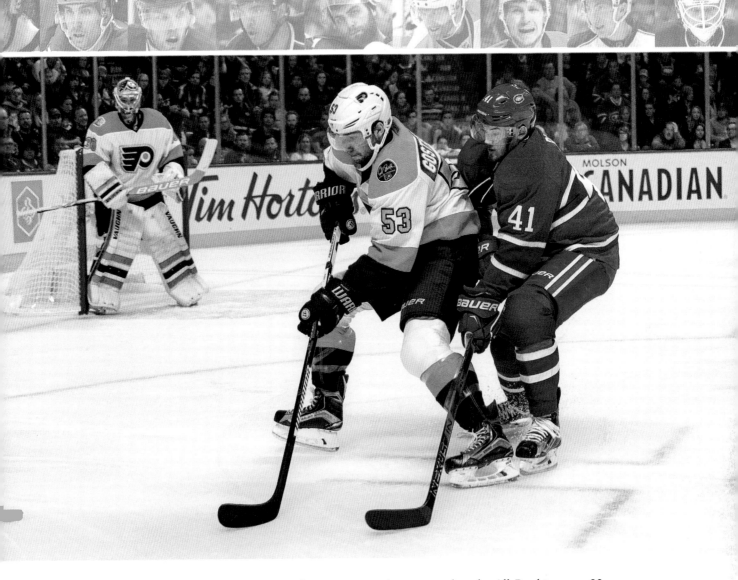

Lehigh Valley Phantoms of the American Hockey League, Gostisbehere tore his ACL and was lost for a year. He started the 2015–16 season with the Phantoms and finished it with the Flyers, coming in second for the Calder Trophy. "It definitely caught me by surprise," said Gostisbehere. "Nobody goes into their first few NHL games and expects to make such a splash. It was a great experience … a lot of fun."

Still undersized, Gostisbehere used his speed and creativity to score 17 goals and 46 points, which was 17th among NHL defensemen. Eighteen of those points came during a 15-game point streak, the longest by a rookie defenseman in NHL history and matching the longest by any defenseman since Chris Chelios in 1995. The last point of the streak was an overtime winner against the Toronto Maple Leafs, which made him the first rookie in history to score four overtime goals in a season.

Gostisbehere played in the 2016 All-Star Game and was named to the All-Rookie team. He was selected for the 23-and-under Team North America squad at the 2016 World Cup of Hockey, where he had four assists to tie for the team lead in points.

In his second season, however, Gostisbehere came back down to earth, a victim of the dreaded sophomore slump. The rookie phenom ended up watching games from the press box as a healthy scratch before picking up his play late in the season. "I learned a lot about myself, not only as a player on the ice, but off the ice, too," said Gostisbehere. "Just getting through hard times, battling through adversity and just coming back and getting back in the groove of things."

The first NHL player born and raised in South Florida already sounds like a grizzled veteran. "I've had the ups and the downs and teetering in the middle again," he said. "So the young guys … if they want to bounce some ideas off me, I'll let them know.

"Because I've got some wisdom now."

SETH JONES

Ronald "Popeye" Jones was a journeyman basketball player, which took him through six NBA cities, including one year in Denver as a Nugget. It was there that his sons fell in love with the game of hockey.

His eldest son, Justin, was the first who wanted to play, but once 6-year-old Seth saw the Colorado Avalanche in Game 7 of the Stanley Cup Final, he was hooked. "They won the Cup there in 2001 and I was able to go to that game," said Seth. "It was Ray Bourque's first Cup and Sakic passed it to him. That jumped up my love for the game.... You don't get many chances to go to a Stanley Cup game and that was a special one."

Knowing more about the hardwood than the ice,

Popeye sought advice from Avalanche captain and fellow Pepsi Center tenant Joe Sakic. "He looked and saw how tall I was," recalled Papa Jones. "Joe wasn't a big guy. He said, 'By the looks of you, they are going to be very tall. Make sure they know how to skate.' I told my boys, 'Joe Sakic said you better know how to skate. You have to be a great skater.'"

So Popeye put Justin, Seth and his youngest son, Caleb, into figure skating, and as Seth grew into his 6-foot-4, 220-pound frame he remained a smooth and efficient skater.

If Popeye couldn't impart hockey wisdom on his sons, he could share the lessons he learned through his fascination with the structure of chess and the value of being a good teammate. "Control the middle of the ice the way you control the middle of the board and think two or three moves ahead of everyone," Popeye advised. "See what board awareness does? Learn ice awareness."

Seth took to the game quickly, choosing defense because he could see the whole ice and control play strategically. He won his first national title in peewee with the Littleton (Colorado) Hawks. "When he was 12, you'd think he was an 18-year-old, the way he comported himself," said Hawks coach Kent Murphy. "He never made anybody feel like he was our best player, which he was. But he made them feel like the team would be better because they were there."

After two years with the U.S. National Team Development Program, during which he won back-to-back gold medals at the Under-18 World Championship, Jones played for the Western Hockey League's Portland Winterhawks, where he won the Jim Piggott Memorial Trophy as WHL Rookie of the Year in 2012–13. He was the number one ranked skater heading into the 2013 NHL entry draft, and most experts assumed the top pick was either going to be Jones or the Halifax Mooseheads' Nathan MacKinnon.

Jones' Team USA won gold at the 2013 World Junior tournament, beating MacKinnon and Canada in the semifinals. Jones was the youngest player on the roster but led the U.S. in plus-minus (plus-8) and average ice time (25:38). "He has it all: size, smarts, skill and a great, great head for the game," said Phil Housley, a Hall of Fame defenseman and Jones' coach at the tournament. "He reminds me a little of Larry Robinson when he was in Montreal. He's the total package."

MacKinnon's Mooseheads beat Jones and the Winterhawks in the 2013 Memorial Cup final, and while a return to Colorado as the first overall pick would have been a nice narrative for Jones, the Avalanche took MacKinnon with the top pick instead. Somewhat surprisingly, Jones fell to the Nashville Predators at fourth.

Jones was stuck behind righties Shea Weber and Ryan Ellis on the depth chart of Nashville defensemen, so on January 6, 2016, he was traded to the Columbus Blue Jackets for center Ryan Johansen in a rare 1-for-1 blockbuster deal.

After playing with MacKinnon on Team North America at the 2016 World Cup of Hockey, Jones had his best NHL season in 2016–17 when he set career highs in goals (12) and points (42) as part of a young Blue Jackets team that finished fourth overall. He averaged 23:24 minutes a game and represented Columbus in his first All-Star Game. "He's a great player," said the Calgary Flames' Johnny Gaudreau, who played with Jones at the World Juniors and World Cup of Hockey. "Smart, skilled, great defensively. He's a great guy off the ice, too, which makes it even better. I love playing with him. It's great to see how well he's doing this year."

Won gold at the 2011 and 2012 Under-18 World Championships

Won gold at the 2013 World Junior Championship

Named WHL Rookie of the Year in 2013

Played in the 2017 NHL All-Star Game

BRADEN HOLTBY

Tied the single season record for wins in 2015–16 (48)

Won the Vezina Trophy in 2016

Won the William Jennings Trophy twice (2016, 2017)

Won the 2016 World Cup of Hockey

Played in two NHL All-Star Games (2016, 2017)

G oaltenders are generally known to be weird. Quirks and superstitions are bred in the solitude of the crease. The mind has extra time to operate whenever the puck is in the other end of the rink, so success often comes down to taming it.

Among the eccentrics of the goalie fraternity, Braden Holtby seems odd in his normalcy. But still waters run deep. "He's a competitive freak," according to former Capitals teammate Michael Latta. "Then off the ice he's such a nice, relaxed guy. Chill, really into music and really cool."

The hockey genes came from his father, Greg, who was a goalie with the Western Hockey League's Saskatoon Blades; the music came from his mother, Tami, who was the winner of the Saskatchewan Female Vocalist of the Year award in 1996.

In Lloydminster, Saskatchewan, the Holtby farm often doubled as a rehearsal space. After practicing, Tami's bandmates would take shots on Braden, because that's all he ever wanted to do.

Having exhausted his supply of goalie knowledge when his son was 15, Greg hired goalie coach and sports psychologist John Stevenson. Braden was talented but prone to temper tantrums, so Stevenson's grasp of the mental game was a helpful bonus.

In 2006 Braden followed his father's footsteps to Saskatoon to backstop the Blades. In his first two seasons as a starter Holtby had a mediocre 42-58-11 record, and he didn't get selected until the fourth round of the 2008 entry draft, when the Washington Capitals chose him 93rd overall. Buoyed by their belief in him, he had a 40-16-4 record in 2008–09 and led the Blades to the playoffs for the first time in three years.

Holtby spent three seasons with the American Hockey League's Hershey Bears, where he earned his nickname Holtbeast, before he got a real shot with the Capitals. He proved he belonged in the 2012 playoffs, with a 1.95 goals-against average and .935 save percentage in 14 games, which included a first round win over the defending champion Boston Bruins.

In 2013–14, Holtby, still fighting for the number one job, was struggling, so Stevenson was called in to help. His training included white pucks and a machine called the CogniSens NeuroTracker to hone mental processing and peripheral vision. He also taught Holtby how to refocus during games, leading to his habit of squirting water after giving up a goal and watching one droplet hit the ice.

In 2014–15 Holtby led the NHL in games played (73) and saves (1,887), and finished second in wins (41). He had nine shutouts, tied for the most in team history, and twice broke the franchise record for consecutive games played.

The Capitals signed Holtby to a five-year, $30.5 million deal, and in 2015–16 his 48 wins tied Martin Brodeur's single season record, in 12 fewer games. He also had a 2.20 goals-against average and .922 save percentage to win the Vezina Trophy.

After a second consecutive Presidents' Trophy for the Capitals in 2016–17, Holtby won the William Jennings Trophy and was a finalist for the Vezina again. His 42 wins tied for the league lead, he was first with nine shutouts and his goals-against average (2.07) and save percentage (.925) were both an improvement on the previous year.

For the third straight season the Capitals bowed out in the second round, but the playoff disappointments can't be laid at Holtby's feet. He has a career 2.00 goals-against average and .932 save percentage in the postseason.

Holtby, who had a tribute to the Canadian rock band The Tragically Hip painted on his mask for the 2016 World Cup of Hockey, also thrives on routine, which includes playing guitar before and after games. "Music just always takes you back to the same place," he explained. "Any type of music, you listen to it, it changes your mood, your outlook on things."

And it soothes the savage Holtbeast.

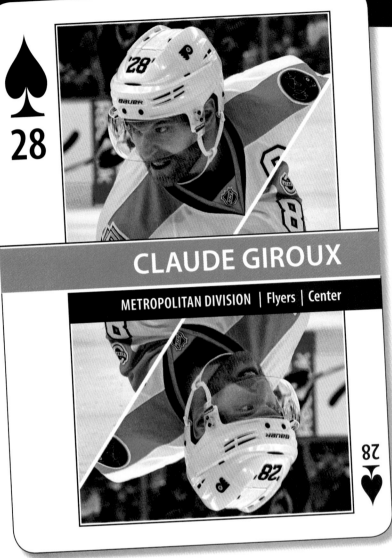

CLAUDE GIROUX

METROPOLITAN DIVISION | Flyers | Center

28

I just wanted to play hockey," Giroux recalled. "My dream was to play in the NHL, but I didn't think I had a chance."

His odds improved greatly when he scored 103 points in the 2005–06 season, and after being drafted he returned to Gatineau and upped his total to 112 points in 2006–07.

The following year Giroux helped Canada win gold at the World Junior Championship, and he capped the season with the Guy Lafleur Trophy as playoff MVP after leading Gatineau to the 2008 QMJHL title.

In 2008–09 Giroux graduated to the American Hockey League's Philadelphia Phantoms where he put up 34 points in 33 games to earn a spot on the Flyers' roster for the second half the season.

Playing in all 82 NHL games in 2009–10, Giroux scored the deciding shootout goal in the season finale against the New York Rangers to send the Flyers to the playoffs. They carried that momentum all the way to the Stanley Cup Final, losing to the Chicago Blackhawks in six games. Giroux had 10 goals and 21 points in 23 playoff games, including the overtime winner in Game 3 of the final.

If that magical spring didn't launch Giroux to the top of the NHL, the following season did. It started with HBO's *24/7* documentary series, which show-cased the Flyers and their young star's sharp tongue. In 2010–11 he hit a career-high 76 points and then bettered it with 93 points in 2011–12, the most by a Flyer since Eric Lindros' 93 in 1998–99. In Game 2 of the second round he set a franchise single-game playoff record with six points, including a hat trick, against the cross-state rival Pittsburgh Penguins.

Giroux's popularity was peaking: his jersey was the top seller on the NHL's website in 2011–12, and he was the cover star of EA Sports' *NHL 13* video game. After the Flyers traded Mike Richards and Jeff Carter

It was an inauspicious start. When called upon to select the 22nd pick of the 2006 entry draft, then-Philadelphia Flyers general manager and former captain Bobby Clarke approached the podium and promptly forgot the name of the player he wanted. It's a good thing he remembered because he was drafting a future star and captain in Claude Giroux.

The undersized center was used to being over-looked. A native of Hearst, Ontario, he was passed over by every Ontario Hockey League team in his draft year.

Undeterred, Giroux walked on with the Gatineau Olympiques of the Quebec Major Junior Hockey League, across the river from Ottawa, where he'd moved when he was 15. "When I went to Gatineau,

the door was then open for Giroux to take a leadership role. On January 15, 2013, he was named the 19th captain in franchise history.

Philadelphia is a notoriously tough sports town, and the DNA of the Broad Street Bullies remains in the Flyers. Giroux was not created in the image of Clarke or Lindros or Chris Pronger, who preceded him as captain. At 5-foot-11 and 185 pounds, he leads by positive example, silky skill instead of brute strength. He's a playmaker, with smarts, creativity and joie de vivre.

"He's kind of this glue guy that keeps everything in perspective," said teammate Matt Read.

Giroux finished third in 2014 Hart Trophy voting, so he was a surprising omission from the 2014 Canadian Olympic team. "He's better than half the guys on that team," said the Flyers' late founder and owner Ed Snider of the snub. "Anybody that thinks that Claude Giroux doesn't belong on the Canadian team, they don't know anything about hockey as far as I'm concerned."

With the maple leaf on his chest, Giroux did win gold at the 2015 World Championship and the title at the 2016 World Cup of Hockey.

The graduate of the Hearst Lumber Kings is also in the hearts and logo of his hometown. Giroux helped fund the Hearst Lumberjacks, a team that debuted in the Northern Ontario Junior Hockey League in 2017. When each player pulls on the black and orange sweater with a crest that features Giroux's initials and number, they'll remember the kid from their remote town who wasn't drafted in major junior but is now one of the NHL's brightest stars.

Won gold at the 2008 World Juniors
Named QMJHL Playoff MVP in 2008
Played in four NHL All-Star Games (2011, 2012, 2015, 2016)
Won gold at the 2015 World Championship
Won the 2016 World Cup of Hockey

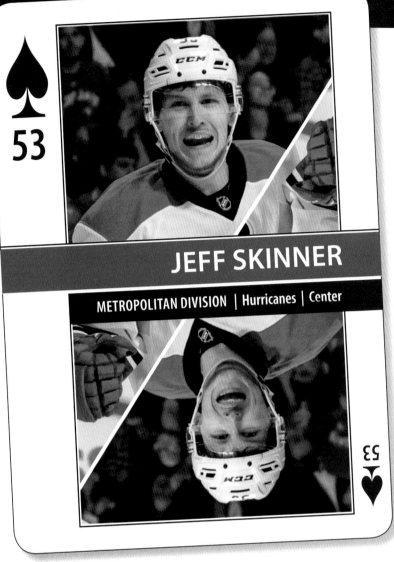

JEFF SKINNER

METROPOLITAN DIVISION | Hurricanes | Center

The 2010 entry draft was all about the Taylor/ Tyler decision, the choice between two blue-chip prospects, who finished the season tied for the Ontario Hockey League scoring title, for first overall.

With top pick Taylor Hall trying to play 18-year-old messiah with the Edmonton Oilers and Tyler Seguin low on the depth chart of a strong Boston Bruins team, another OHL grad quietly skated up the middle.

The seventh overall selection, Jeff Skinner scored 31 goals and 63 points for the Carolina Hurricanes to win the Calder Trophy as rookie of the year in 2011. He didn't turn 19 until the season was over, which made him the youngest Calder winner in

NHL history, as well as the youngest to play in an All-Star Game in any of North America's four major team sports.

Skinner had been ready for primetime since he was a kid. At the age of 9 he had a role in the Robin Williams movie *Death to Smoochy*, and when he was 11 he won the bronze medal at the Skate Canada Junior Nationals, a competition that included future two-time Olympic silver medalist Patrick Chan.

A little healthy sibling rivalry didn't hurt his development either. Parents Elisabeth and Andrew, both lawyers and athletes of the year in law school, had six competitive children who all did figure skating, power skating, swimming, gymnastics, piano lessons and dance classes, to name a few activities. But hockey was the family's first love. "We were literally at the rink almost every day, and if we weren't playing, we were watching," Skinner said of his childhood in Markham, Ontario. "It was hectic, [but] we all knew how important it was to have someone in the stands."

Despite his figure skating background, Skinner's skating was questioned leading up to the draft, but the Hurricanes knew what he was capable of. "He is a driven competitor who is very mature for his age," said Jason Karmanos, Carolina's assistant general manager when Skinner was drafted. "The fact that Jeff is part of a family of high achievers certainly helped cement the opinion within our organization that he had the character and work ethic necessary to succeed at the highest level of the game."

Did he ever. "It is special to come into the NHL and score 30-plus goals," said Paul Maurice, Skinner's coach during his rookie year. "It usually takes three, four or even five years to develop. Everyone down here has fallen in love with him. He is grounded and he looks like he's having fun."

Concussions have cost Skinner games and points

since his rookie season; he missed 16 games in his second year, and after scoring 33 goals in 2013–14 he suffered a third concussion in four years in 2014–15. But Skinner recovered and returned to form in 2015–16, scoring 14 goals in the final 18 games to lead the Hurricanes in points, with 51, for the first time. "I think he took huge strides and really stepped up down the stretch," said general manager Ron Francis. "I thought he became more interested in the 200-foot game and leading by example."

Already a savvy six-year veteran at 24, Skinner was

named an alternate captain before the 2016–17 season. According to Francis, "He was working extremely hard and calling guys out when they weren't doing things the right way, and we felt he had grown into the leadership role.

"He's wise beyond his years in how he trains, eats and takes care of himself. He's a very smart player and understands the game well."

Skinner led the Hurricanes in scoring again and he was sixth in the NHL with 37 goals and second with 30 even-strength goals. He's the fresh face of the franchise, a mix of hard-earned NHL experience and youthful enthusiasm. "Just a kid who loves the game," is how he is described by goalie Cam Ward, a frequent victim of Skinner's pranks.

Teammate Lee Stempniak agreed: "He's funny and he's got a great personality. He enjoys life and has that mischievous grin all the time."

Selected seventh overall in the 2010 NHL entry draft

Won the Calder Trophy in 2011

Played in the 2011 NHL All-Star Game

Was the Hurricanes scoring leader twice (2015–16, 2016–17)

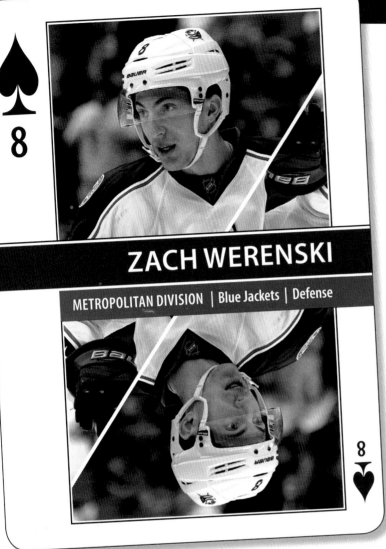

ZACH WERENSKI

METROPOLITAN DIVISION | Blue Jackets | Defense

Zach Werenski was determined to enter college a year early so he completed his entire senior year of high school in one summer. The native of Grosse Pointe, Michigan, had already started at the University of Michigan when he returned home to write one last exam. "Thank God I passed and I got into school, but it was pretty crazy," said Werenski.

At 17, Werenski was the youngest player in the NCAA, yet he was already 6-foot-2 and over 200 pounds as a freshman. He led the Wolverines defense in scoring and the conference in goals among defensemen, and was named to the All-Big Ten first team as well as the Big Ten All-Freshman team. "He looked like a senior, just the way he was built," said Maple Leafs' Zach Hyman of his former Michigan teammate.

It wasn't just his size that impressed. The Werenskis were devoted Detroit Red Wings fans, and Zach grew up admiring Nicklas Lidstrom, particularly his calmness with the puck, which he brought to his own game.

The Columbus Blue Jackets liked his combination of size and serenity and drafted Werenski eighth overall in 2015.

Returning to Michigan for his sophomore season, he ranked second in scoring among all NCAA defenders and captained the bronze medal–winning Team USA at the 2016 World Juniors. He led all defensemen with nine points and all skaters with a plus-10 rating en route to being named the best defenseman and a media all-star.

Forgoing his last two years of college, Werenski got his first taste of professional hockey toward the end of the 2015–16 American Hockey League season. He joined the Lake Erie Monsters for the last seven games of the regular season and the playoffs. The Monsters won the Calder Cup and Werenski had nine assists and 14 points in 17 postseason games. He ranked second among AHL defensemen in playoff scoring, with the most assists and points by an 18-year-old in AHL playoff history.

There was nothing left for Werenski to conquer but the NHL, and in 2016–17 the rookie had 47 points in 78 games, with a plus-17 rating and only 14 penalty minutes.

The second-youngest defenseman in the NHL (behind the Arizona Coyotes' Jakob Chychrun), Werenski was the top scorer among rookie blue-liners, seventh in overall rookie scoring and had the sixth-most points by a rookie teenage defenseman in NHL history. He set a Blue Jackets record for points by a rookie, which was also the second-most points by a defenseman in franchise history.

Werenski averaged almost 21 minutes per game

and had the best possession rating of all Blue Jackets defensemen. He helped the team to a 16-game winning streak, one shy of the NHL record, and a 50-win, 108-point season.

The 2016–17 season ended a little more painfully, however. Werenski missed the last four games of the regular season after a crunching bodycheck from Alex Ovechkin, and in the third game of the playoffs against the Pittsburgh Penguins, a Phil Kessel shot rode up his stick and hit him in the face, leading to a right eye that was 50 shades of black and swollen shut.

After trying to play with a full visor, Werenski was taken out of the game and declared finished for the season, which ended two games later when Columbus was eliminated. "Balls as big as the building," is how Blue Jackets coach John Tortorella described Werenski's effort to return to the game.

Werenski was a finalist for the Calder Trophy in one of the strongest seasons for rookies in NHL history, so

his first year won't be remembered just for the size of his black eye or anything else on his anatomy. "He makes everything look easy, even to the point where people almost think he's lackadaisical, but that's definitely not the case," said Maple Leaf and Calder Trophy winner Auston Matthews, who met Werenski at a tryout camp when the two were 15 and played with him on the U.S. World Junior team. Asked how Werenski does it, Matthews replied, "I don't know honestly, he's ridiculous. He's gross."

And he's not just talking about his face.

Named a First Team All-American and Big Ten Defensive Player of the Year in 2016
Won bronze at the 2016 World Junior Championship and named best defenseman
Voted a finalist for the Calder Trophy in 2017
Set the Blue Jackets record for points by a rookie

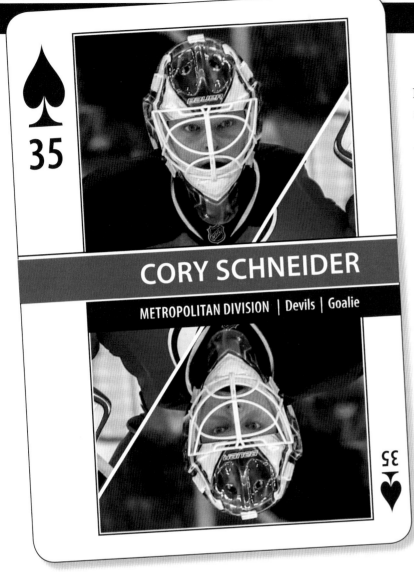

CORY SCHNEIDER

METROPOLITAN DIVISION | Devils | Goalie

National Team Development Program. "It was a little surreal back then," recalled Schneider. "It was a really big deal when I got the call. You go to a tournament where everything was regionalized, team New England, team Michigan, and then you take the best of the best for the national team. That was the pinnacle, putting that USA jersey on for the first time. It was an amazing experience. I couldn't believe I got selected."

Schneider helped the U.S. win gold at the 2003 Under-18 Junior World Cup and silver at the 2004 Under-18 World Championship. After being chosen 26th overall by the Vancouver Canucks in 2004, he played three seasons at Boston College, backstopping the Eagles to consecutive Hockey East titles and trips to the NCAA title game. He also represented his country at the 2005 and 2006 World Juniors.

Schneider spent most of the next three years in the American Hockey League before joining Roberto Luongo in the Vancouver crease in 2010–11. In their first year together the tandem combined to win the William Jennings Trophy for fewest goals against in the NHL. In their second year a goalie controversy was born.

The two shared the duties evenly throughout the season. While there was no personal animosity, the situation quickly became untenable. After Schneider took over for Luongo during the 2012 playoffs, the latter asked to be traded. That wasn't so easy; Luongo had a 12-year, $64 million contract, and no team was willing to take that on. So they spent 2012–13 as uncomfortable bedfellows.

At this point Luongo was 34, had eight years remaining and a no-trade clause, while Schneider was 26 with two years left on his contract. Vancouver's then-general manager Mike Gillis found a willing partner in the New Jersey Devils and traded

In the power struggle for the lone position in every NHL crease, Cory Schneider has staged two bloodless coups, unseating two Hall of Fame-bound goalies along the way.

Not bad for a kid from Marblehead, Massachusetts, with no history of hockey in the family. It was only because his older brother, Geoff, played that Cory tagged along. Always willing to take shots from his brother at home, Schneider first took a turn at goalie like everyone else on his team. He eventually alternated with one other player, each playing one game in net and one as a forward, until he took over the job of number one goalie, as he tends to do.

It wasn't until Schneider was a high school senior at Phillips Academy that he was asked to join the U.S.

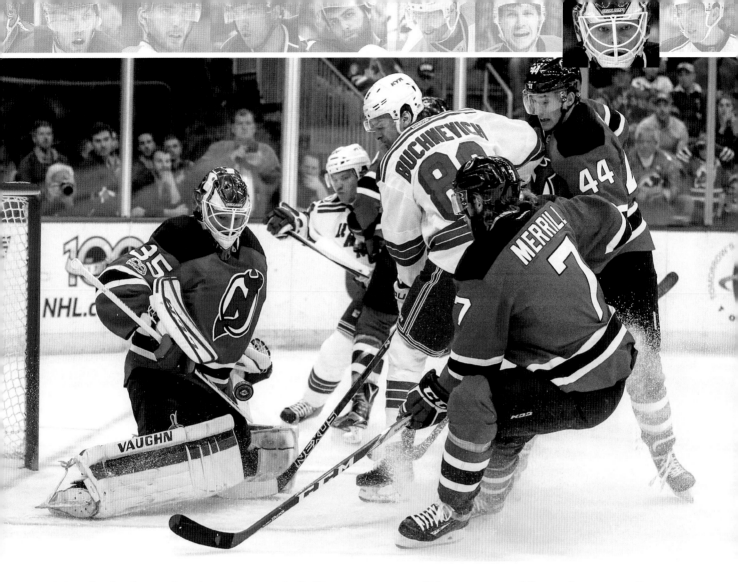

Schneider for the ninth pick in the 2013 draft. "It was shocking," said Schneider. "In the first few years I always sort of assumed that I was going to get dealt at some point. But then drafts and trade deadlines went by and nothing ever happened. With the extension last year I kind of felt, finally I had kind of gotten away from the trade rumors."

In New Jersey Schneider went from sharing duties with the man who had the second-most wins by any active goalie to the one with the most of all-time. Martin Brodeur is arguably the best to ever don the pads, and Schneider was brought in to replace him.

In 2014 the Devils signed Schneider to a seven-year, $42 million contract that will keep him in New Jersey through the 2021–22 season. That spelled the end for the 42-year-old Brodeur after 21 seasons, three Stanley Cups and four Vezina Trophies. "We had a decision to move going forward with Cory," said Lou Lamoriello, then-president and general

manager. "Marty was excited for us when we got Cory and has tremendous respect for him as an individual. We're going from one great goaltender to another."

Finally a true number-one NHL goalie, Schneider was philosophical: "I'm not looking at this as I'm replacing Marty Brodeur. I think I'm more continuing the legacy of great goaltending in New Jersey." With a .922 career save percentage at the end of the 2016–17 season, the third-highest in NHL history, it's hard to argue with that.

Won gold at the 2003 Under-18 Junior World Cup and silver at the 2004 Under-18 World Championship

Named the AHL's Best Goaltender in 2009

Won the William Jennings Trophy in 2011

Played in the 2016 NHL All-Star Game

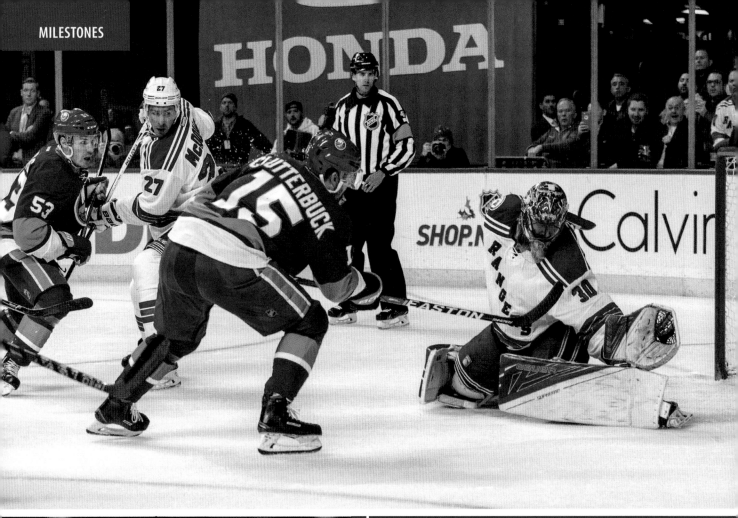

HENRIK LUNDQVIST

METROPOLITAN DIVISION | Rangers | Goalie | 30

- Won gold at the 2002 Inline Hockey World Championship
- Won silver at the 2003 and 2004 World Championships
- Named Swedish Elite League Goalie of the Year in 2003, 2004 and 2005
- Awarded the Guldpucken (Golden Puck) as Sweden's best hockey player in 2005
- Awarded the Guldhjalmen (Golden Helmet) as Sweden's played-voted MVP in 2005
- Won gold at the 2006 Olympics and silver at the 2014 Olympics
- Led the NHL in shutouts in 2007–08 (10) and 2010–11 (11)
- Played in three NHL All-Star Games (2009, 2011, 2012)
- Won the Vezina Trophy in 2012
- Won gold at the 2017 World Championship

"King Henrik" Lundqvist is not ready to abdicate his throne. In 2016–17 a young Finn attempted to topple him — Antti Raanta had a 16-8-2 record, 2.26 goals-against average and .922 save percentage, nearly taking the New York Rangers' number one job — but Lundqvist survived the coup d'crease and added some major milestones to an already impressive list of accomplishments.

Lundqvist first strapped on the pads when he was 7, and his twin brother, Joel, volunteered him to backstop their team in Are, a tiny skiing village in northern Sweden. It was love at first save, even if he allowed 12 goals in his first game and 18 his second.

Showing some improvement, Lundqvist joined Frolunda, his favorite childhood team, in 2000. After the Rangers took a chance on him in the seventh round (205th overall) of the 2000 entry draft, he won the Honken Trophy as best goalie in the Elitserien (Sweden's top league) three consecutive years from 2003–2005.

In 2004–05 Lundqvist set Swedish records for the longest shutout streak (172:29) in the regular season, and led Frolunda to the championship with a 1.05 goals-against average and .962 save percentage in the playoffs. He won the Guldpucken as league MVP and the Guldhjalmen for player-voted MVP.

Lundqvist made his debut on Broadway in 2005–06 and set a franchise rookie record with 30 victories. He was fourth in the NHL with a .922 save percentage, fifth with a 2.24 goals-against average and a finalist for the Vezina Trophy.

Lundqvist was a Vezina finalist in each of his first three seasons and top six in voting for 10 straight years. He won it in 2011–12 and was a Hart Trophy finalist after going 39-18-5 with a 1.97 goals-against average and .930 save percentage.

Lundqvist has now won 30 or more games 11 times. He is the first goalie in NHL history with 11 straight 20-win seasons and the only one with 30 wins in each full season he's played.

The wins have added up quickly, and on New Year's Eve 2016 he beat the Colorado Avalanche for his 390th, passing Dominik Hasek for most wins by a European-born goaltender in NHL history.

The Avalanche were victims of history again on February 11, 2017, when Lundqvist became the 12th goalie in NHL history with 400 wins. He did it in just 727 games, beating Martin Brodeur, who took 735 games, to set a new NHL record for the quickest to 400. He also joined Brodeur and Tony Esposito as the only goalies to win 400 games with one team.

Entering the 2017–18 season, Lundqvist holds every Rangers goaltending record, including victories (405), shutouts (61), playoff wins (61) and games played (742 in the regular season and 128 in the playoffs). He's second in wins and shutouts among all active goalies behind Roberto Luongo (453 and 73), and his .920 save percentage is eighth all-time.

With a win over the Florida Panthers days after his 35th birthday, Lundqvist passed Grant Fuhr for 10th on the all-time list. If he continues his pace for the remainder of his contract, which runs through 2020–21, he'll reach 500 career wins and be third on the all-time list, behind Brodeur and Patrick Roy.

Lundqvist is still searching for his first Stanley Cup, but he's always been a money goalie under pressure. He set an NHL record with six consecutive Game 7 wins, and he's won just about everything else in hockey, including the 2002 Inline World Championship with Team Sweden. He also earned a gold at the 2006 Olympics and set an Olympic record for longest shutout streak (172:34) that stretched over the 2006 and 2010 Games.

After getting the better of the Montreal Canadiens in the first round of the 2017 playoffs, the Rangers fell to the Ottawa Senators. Following the loss Lundqvist joined Team Sweden at the World Championship.

Henrik was the oldest member of the team, beating Joel, his brother and captain, by a matter of minutes. Joining forces for the first time since their Frolunda days, they beat Canada in a shootout in the gold medal game for another jewel in the King's crown.

Long may he reign.

CENTRAL DIVISION

FIRST STARS

86	**JONATHAN TOEWS**	Blackhawks	Center
88	**PATRICK KANE**	Blackhawks	Right Wing
90	**JAMIE BENN**	Stars	Left Wing
92	**DUNCAN KEITH**	Blackhawks	Defense
94	**P.K. SUBBAN**	Predators	Defense
96	**PEKKA RINNE**	Predators	Goalie

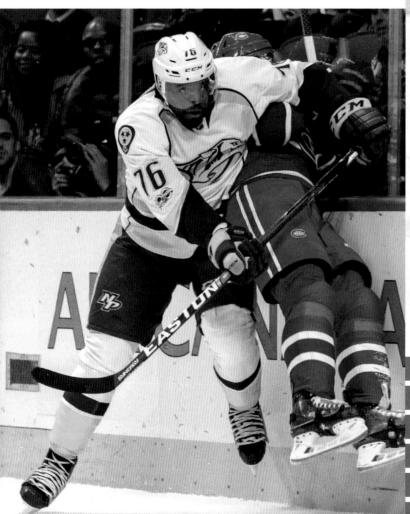

SECOND STARS

98	**TYLER SEGUIN**	Stars	Center
100	**PATRIK LAINE**	Jets	Right Wing
102	**VLADIMIR TARASENKO**	Blues	Right Wing
104	**ALEX PIETRANGELO**	Blues	Defense
106	**RYAN SUTER**	Wild	Defense
108	**DEVAN DUBNYK**	Wild	Goalie

BLACK ACES

MILESTONES

JONATHAN TOEWS

Even his parents knew early on. "If I had not seen him being born, I would swear he's older," said his mother, Andrée Gilbert. And according to his father, Bryan, "He had been skating by the time he was three-and-a-half and had a stride at four. That blew my mind."

Jonathan Toews matured quickly, with an adult's intensity long before puberty. Growing up in the St. Vital neighborhood in south Winnipeg, his team of 7-year-olds lost a tournament game to a team a year older. "He was so upset," said Bryan. "I tried to explain that the other team was all older boys, but he didn't accept that. He wanted to beat them."

Toews had the talent to match. He was chosen first overall in the 2003 Western Hockey League draft by the Tri-City Americans but decided to attend Shattuck-St. Mary's, the Minnesota prep school that produced Sidney Crosby, because it was closer to home and he'd remain eligible to play in the NCAA.

Serious about school, too, Toews completed three years of high school in two and enrolled at the University of North Dakota in 2005 at 17. He had 85 points in 76 games over two seasons with the Fighting Sioux and won gold at the World Junior Championship with Canada both years.

The second, in 2007, will long be remembered for the win over Team USA in the semifinals, when Toews had three goals in three attempts in a seven-round shootout. "He was so cool. Maybe on the inside, something else was going on, but not on the outside," said coach Craig Hartsburg. "And that's why he's a great captain and a great leader."

Toews was drafted third overall by the Chicago Blackhawks in 2006 and made his NHL debut in 2007 with that year's first overall pick, Patrick Kane. One prescient scout predicted Kane would one day lead the NHL in scoring, which he did, while Toews would lead the Blackhawks to the Stanley Cup, which he's done three times.

After being dubbed Mr. Serious by his Chicago teammates, Toews was upgraded to Captain Serious in 2008. He'd played only 64 NHL games and was the third-youngest captain in league history at the time.

Invited to Canada's Olympic orientation camp in 2009, Toews still wasn't sure he belonged: "I'm watching Sidney Crosby, a young captain like myself, and it's pretty incredible to see a guy who's about my age doing the things he's doing. I get praise for things that are modest compared to what he's done."

When the 2010 Olympics rolled around, Crosby got most of the headlines and the Golden Goal, but Toews led Canada in scoring and was named the tournament's best forward. A few months later he had 29 points in 22 playoff games to win the Stanley Cup, the Blackhawks' first in 49 years. He became the second-youngest captain to lift the Cup, after Crosby, and the second-youngest player to be named playoff MVP, after Patrick Roy, when he was voted the Conn Smythe Trophy winner. He also became the youngest player in history to join the Triple Gold Club, with his Stanley Cup, Olympic gold and World Championship gold, which he'd won in 2007.

The general manager of the Olympic team was Steve Yzerman, the first ballot Hall of Famer whom Toews is most frequently compared to. Toews was an easy choice because Yzerman sees a lot of himself in him, except that "Jonathan's bigger, stronger, better ... faster. He just is a tremendous all-around player."

Over 22 seasons Yzerman won three Stanley Cups, one Conn Smythe and one Selke. After winning two more Cups in 2013 and 2015, Toews had done all of that by the end of his eighth season. His Selke Trophy as best defensive forward came in 2013, and he added the Mark Messier Leadership Award in 2015. Not finished he took home more gold at the 2014 Olympics and won the 2016 World Cup of Hockey.

In 2016–17, at his sixth All-Star Game, Toews was named one of the NHL's 100 Greatest Players, one of just six active players.

In the off-season Toews, who has a lake in Manitoba named after him, took to Instagram to voice his concerns about climate change. In a dicey political climate it was a bold move for an athlete, but for Captain Serious there are larger issues than the Blackhawks' first round loss in 2017, and that conviction and integrity define a true leader.

Won gold at the 2006 and 2007 World Juniors, 2007 World Championship, 2010 and 2014 Olympics, and won the 2016 World Cup of Hockey

Won the Stanley Cup three times (2010, 2013, 2015)

Won the Conn Smythe Trophy in 2010

Awarded the Frank J. Selke Trophy in 2013

Received the Mark Messier Leadership Award in 2015

PATRICK KANE

Won the Calder Trophy in 2008

Played in six NHL All-Star Games (2009, 2011, 2012, 2015, 2016, 2017)

Won the Stanley Cup three times (2010, 2013, 2015)

Won the Conn Smythe Trophy in 2013

Won the Hart Trophy, Art Ross Trophy and Ted Lindsay Award in 2016

P atrick Kane is the product of working-class South Buffalo, where there's a "special culture," according to NHL icon Scotty Bowman, former coach and general manager of the Sabres. "If you're from South Buffalo — or you're accepted there — you're a different kind of guy."

Generously listed at 5-foot-11 and 177 pounds now, Kane was always the smallest and usually the best on his team. By the age of 11, he was putting up 230 points in a 60-game season. At 14, having left home, he had 160 points in 70 games for the Detroit HoneyBaked AAA team in 2002–03. Twice cut by the U.S. National Team Development Program because of his size, Kane broke a program record in his second season with 102 points in 58 games. In 2006–07, his lone season in the Ontario Hockey League, he had 62 goals and 145 points in 58 games for the London Knights. He was both the Canadian Hockey League's leading scorer and Rookie of the Year.

After being drafted first overall by the Chicago Blackhawks in 2007, Kane stepped right into the NHL and scored his first career goal against former Sabre and his childhood idol Dominik Hasek. He finished the 2007–08 season with 21 goals and 72 points to win the Calder Trophy. It was the Blackhawks' first winning season in six years and the start of a resurgence that culminated in the team's first Stanley Cup in nearly half a century.

In 2010 Kane had 10 goals and 28 points in 22 playoff games, the last of which in Game 6 against the Philadelphia Flyers made him the youngest player to score the Stanley Cup–winning goal in overtime.

In 2013 Kane had a hat trick against the Los Angeles Kings that included the double-overtime winner to clinch the Western Conference Final, and his second goal in Game 5 of the Stanley Cup Final against the Boston Bruins was also the game-winner. He won the Conn Smythe Trophy and his second Stanley Cup, and in 2015 he came back from a broken collarbone to score 23 points in 23 playoff games and win his third Cup.

Addressing the crowd at the celebration in Chicago, Kane said ominously, "I know you've said I've been growing up, but watch out for me the next week."

In August 2015 Kane was accused of sexual assault at his lake house outside of Buffalo. While the district attorney declined to press charges it wasn't forgotten in opposing rinks, especially in his hometown.

Kane had pleaded guilty to non-criminal disorderly conduct as a result of assaulting a cab driver in 2009, and the people of Buffalo had run out of patience with their wayward child and weren't afraid to voice it when the Blackhawks came to town.

Either Kane is as adept at compartmentalizing, or the anger directed at him was motivation in 2015–16. He had a 26-game point streak, the longest since Mats Sundin's 30 straight in 1992–93, and in his lone game in Buffalo he tied the score with 35.9 seconds left and then beat the Sabres with a shootout goal.

After leading the NHL that season with 106 points (46 goals, 60 assists), 17 more than second-place Jamie Benn, Kane became the first U.S.-born player to win the Art Ross and Hart Trophies. He completed the hat trick with the Ted Lindsay Award.

Entering the 2017–18 season, Kane has 752 points in 740 career games, and 123 points in 127 career playoff games. Of his 50 playoff goals, 11 were game-winners, the most in Blackhawks postseason history, and his five playoff overtime goals tie him with Glenn Anderson for third in history, behind Joe Sakic (eight) and Maurice Richard (six).

These are the reasons Kane was named one of the NHL's 100 Greatest Players in 2017. One of only six active players to make the list, at 29 he's still just hitting the sweet spot where the peak of his abilities meets the wisdom of life's hard lessons, some of which he's brought upon himself.

South Buffalo's prodigal son has not wasted his talent, now he's working on earning forgiveness.

JAMIE BENN

I n an era of specialization, Jamie Benn is the last of a dying breed of well-rounded athletes.

Benn grew up in Victoria, British Columbia. He was just 5-foot-3 in 10th grade so it didn't look like he'd amount to much on either the ice or the baseball diamond, his two seasonal passions. But a growth spurt eventually came, and he was named MVP when his midget AAA baseball team, the Victoria Capitals, won the provincial title in 2006. His coach said he was the second-best left-handed hitter to come out of Victoria after former Major League Baseball star Michael Saunders.

"My dad was a big promoter of when it's hockey season you play hockey, but when it's baseball season you play baseball," said brother Jordie, a former teammate on the Dallas Stars and now a Montreal Canadien. "Just let the kids figure out what they want to do. He never pushed us to do anything, he just wanted us to choose. So when it came to that time, he was happy that we chose hockey. He doesn't know where the hockey talent came from because he wasn't a hockey player, but it just kind of worked out."

Benn didn't focus on hockey until after high school, which might be why a scouting report before the 2007 NHL entry draft said: "We're not sure if he's really that slow, or he just refuses to move."

Playing for the Tier II Victoria Grizzlies in the British Columbia Hockey League he wasn't a high profile prospect, but he had 42 goals and 65 points in 53 games, and the Dallas Stars took a chance on him in the fifth round, 129th overall. After being drafted Benn tried out for the Western Hockey League's Kelowna Rockets, made the team and committed to hockey exclusively for the first time. "After I got drafted I kind of took [hockey] more seriously," said Benn. "I had a lot of great help in Kelowna playing for the Rockets, and finally figured out it was going to take a lot of hard work to get to the NHL."

Benn had 79 goals and 147 points in 107 games over two seasons in Kelowna, and led the team to the Memorial Cup in 2009. The Rockets lost in the final, but Benn took home the Ed Chynoweth Award as the tournament's leading scorer. He also won gold with Canada at the 2009 World Junior Championship.

Benn went straight from junior to the NHL and had 22 goals and 19 assists in 2009–10. His offense took off when the Stars traded for center Tyler Seguin in 2013, allowing Benn, who was named captain a few months later, to move to left wing. The chemistry between the two was instant, and Benn has averaged over a point per game since.

During his first season alongside Seguin, Benn was selected by Team Canada for the 2014 Sochi Olympics. Wise choice, as he scored the only goal in a 1-0 semifinal win over Team USA on the way to the gold medal.

In 2014 Sidney Crosby and Patrick Kane called Benn the NHL's most underrated player, a prescient vote as he won the 2015 Art Ross Trophy as the league's scoring leader with 87 points (35 goals, 52 assists). The following season he had a career-high 89 points (41 goals, 48 assists), finishing second to Kane and joining Kane and Crosby as the three Hart Trophy finalists for league MVP in 2016.

Now 6-foot-2 and 210 pounds, Benn's game is more than just point production. The captain led the Stars with 120 hits in 2014–15 and 156 in 2015–16 and ranked first among Stars forwards in blocked shots with 59 in 2013–14 and second with 55 in 2015–16. "He's unbelievable," said former Stars teammate Alex Goligoski. "He can play the game any way you want to play it. If it's a real hard-nosed game, he can be the best player on the ice, and if it's an up-and-down skill game, he can be the best player on the ice. For me, if I'm starting a team, he's probably the guy I want on it right now."

Ranked fourth in the NHL Network's list of the top 50 players prior to the 2016–17 season, the Stars have locked Benn up with an eight-year, $76 million contract that runs through 2024–25. The late bloomer might just reach number one on the list by then.

Won gold at the 2009 World Junior Championship

Played in two NHL All-Star Games (2012, 2016)

Won gold at the 2014 Olympics

Won the Art Ross Trophy in 2015

Voted a Hart Trophy finalist in 2016

DUNCAN KEITH

Played in four NHL All-Star Games (2008, 2011, 2015, 2017)

Won gold at the 2010 and 2014 Olympics

Won the Stanley Cup three times (2010, 2013, 2015)

Won the Norris Trophy twice (2010, 2014)

Won the Conn Smythe Trophy in 2015

For a kid born in Manitoba, who moved to northern Ontario and then British Columbia, Chicago is a great place to end up.

Duncan Keith is notoriously private, so being in one of America's biggest, sports-heavy cities, while having two of the NHL's best forwards on his team to absorb the spotlight, suits him fine.

What is known about Keith is that his parents keep a framed piece of paper on which as a child he wrote, "Duncan Keith will make the NHL," a statement of determination that didn't fade with age.

Playing atom hockey in Fort Frances, Ontario, Keith was asked to play for another local team at a tournament in Minneapolis. "He was pumped," recalled his father, David. "There were teams from all around the world. We played the Moscow Selects, with Ilya Kovalchuk. [Kovalchuk] scored four goals … we lost 7–3. Duncan was distraught. He told us he wanted to move to Russia, so he could get better over there."

The family relocated to Penticton, British Columbia, instead, when Duncan was 15. "As soon as we saw him on the ice, wow," said Penticton Panthers bantam coach Rob McLaughlin. "He was 130 pounds, 5-foot-6. But you couldn't hit or touch him."

Keith was still on the small side when the time came to take the next step, so he chose to play at Michigan State University instead of the more physical Western Hockey League. It was at preseason fitness training in 2001 that another piece of Keith's lore was born. "He looked like a track athlete, skinny and young. I don't want to say his numbers were exactly like Lance Armstrong's, but that was the comparison they used," said former MSU teammate and current NHLer John-Michael Liles.

Keith left the Spartans in his sophomore year to join the WHL's Kelowna Rockets for the latter half of the 2002–03 season. He joined future NHL star Shea Weber in the defense corps, and the Rockets went 16-3 in the playoffs to win the WHL title.

The blue-liner still wasn't a blue chip prospect, however. Keith was the 16th defenseman drafted in

2002 when the Blackhawks chose him in the second round, 54th overall, and he spent two years with the American Hockey League's Norfolk Admirals before he fulfilled his childhood promise in 2005.

Over his first five seasons Keith's responsibilities and reputation grew every year, as did his point totals. In 2010 he led a stacked Team Canada in ice time at the Vancouver Olympics en route to a gold medal.

It was the start of one of the best stretches a player has ever had. Keith added the 2010 Stanley Cup, and after finishing 2009–10 with a career-high 69 points he won his first Norris Trophy.

The Blackhawks added another Cup in 2013, and in 2014 Keith anchored a defense that allowed only three goals in the entire Olympic tournament as Canada won gold in Sochi. As in the previous Olympic year, Keith again earned the Norris Trophy.

For a player still managing to fly under the radar, thanks in part to teammates Patrick Kane and

Jonathan Toews, Keith was hard to miss in 2015. He averaged a mindboggling 31 minutes a night in the playoffs and became the fourth player in NHL history with more than 700 minutes in the postseason (715:37). He led the league with 18 assists, and his 21 points tied Chris Pronger for the most by a defenseman in the past 20 years. His three goals were all game-winners, including the Cup-clincher, and he was the unanimous choice for the Conn Smythe.

From his first NHL season through the end of 2016–17, Keith's 511 points lead all defensemen, and Zdeno Chara is the only blue-liner with a better rating than Keith's plus-172.

Keith played in his fourth All-Star Game in 2017, and as part of the NHL centenary festivities, the league announced its 100 Greatest Players. Only six were active players and Keith was the only active defenseman. Characteristically he deflected: "I'm just lucky to be on a team with such good players."

P.K. SUBBAN

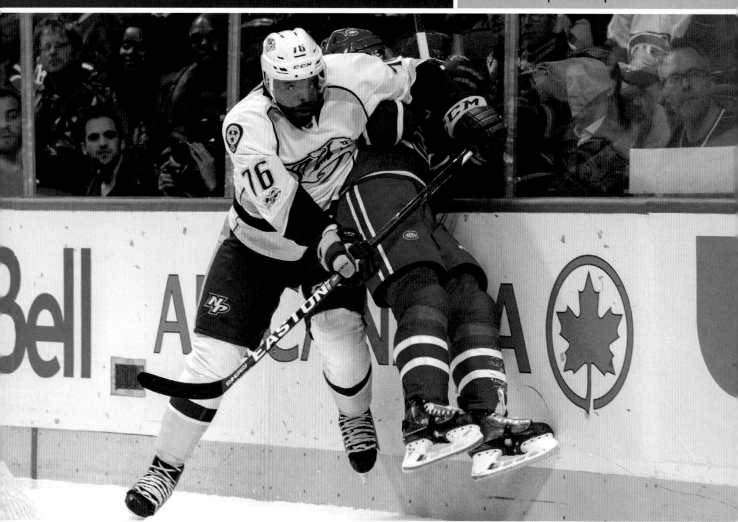

After the Canadiens traded P.K. Subban, a season ticket holder took out a full-page ad in the *Montreal Gazette* to thank him for his service to the team and city. "You are an amazing and influential role model for my children and I am going to miss not having you as a Montreal Canadien," read the open letter from Dr. Charles Kowalski.

Such is the love that Montreal has for one of its favorite sons, the heir to the Flying Frenchman and the most entertaining man in a hidebound sport.

Subban embraced the city right back. He wore the Bleu, Blanc et Rouge with obvious pride, and made a $10 million donation to the Montreal Children's Hospital, a record for a Canadian athlete. Together

with Carey Price he was going to bring the glory back to Les Glorieux.

Until June 29, 2016, when the Canadiens shocked the hockey world by sending Subban to the Nashville Predators for Shea Weber. Montreal general manager Marc Bergevin claimed it was simply an opportunity to upgrade his team, while nebulous stories emerged of discord in the dressing room and a clash with then-coach Michel Therrien.

Subban can be thrilling on the ice, but it's a high-risk, high-reward proposition that doesn't sit well with some coaches, including Mike Babcock, coach of Canada's Olympic teams in 2010 and 2014 and its World Cup of Hockey team in 2016. It's the reason that Subban saw very little ice in Sochi and why he was left off the roster entirely at the World Cup.

Pernell Karl Subban was born and raised in Rexdale, a diverse neighborhood in northwest Toronto, and his father, Karl, used to take him downtown for late-night skates in front of Toronto City Hall. Karl immigrated from Jamaica and his wife, Maria, from Montserrat. P.K. is the one of five children and the oldest of three sons, all of whom went on to the NHL after graduating from the Ontario Hockey League's Belleville Bulls. Over four years he became the franchise's highest scoring defensemen and won two gold medals with Canada at the World Juniors in 2008 and 2009.

After being drafted by the Canadiens 43rd overall in 2007, Subban stormed into the league in the 2010 playoffs and won the Norris Trophy three years later, just a month after turning 24.

The 2014 playoffs were Subban's signature Montreal moment. He had four goals and three assists in a seven game series against the reviled Boston Bruins, including a tide-turning breakaway goal. Before Game 7 in Boston he said, "I can't wait for the crowd, the noise, the energy in the building. I can't wait to take that away from them."

There were plenty who thought he should stick to the usual staid script, but Subban doesn't play that way. "I really don't care what the other team thinks," he said after eliminating the Bruins. "I don't care what their fans think. If they hate me, great. Hate me. We'll just keep winning, I'll keep scoring and we'll move on."

Many expected Subban to be named captain in 2015, but the team voted for Max Pacioretty. Less than a year later Subban was a Predator.

Subban brought his thunderous hip-checks, cannonading slap shots and sartorial splendor to Nashville. By the end of the year he'd led the Predators to their first Stanley Cup Final in franchise history, where they faced the Pittsburgh Penguins.

At the end of Game 3, a Predators win that Subban had guaranteed, he had an on-ice exchange with friend Sidney Crosby. Subban said it involved his bad breath and mouthwash, but it was actually much more mundane and profane than his account.

Critics suggested he'd erred in poking the Crosby bear. Whether or not that was true, Crosby subsequently played his best games of the series and won the Stanley Cup and Conn Smythe Trophy. It may also be the reason Subban didn't speak to the media during the last few days of the final.

Stifling Subban is nearly impossible for foes; for the Predators and the league, it's a waste of megawatt star power and desperately needed originality.

Won gold at the 2008 and 2009 World Junior Championships

Won the Norris Trophy in 2013

Won gold at the 2014 Olympics

Played in two NHL All-Star Games (2016, 2017)

PEKKA RINNE

Wayne Gretzky once said there are three seasons: the regular season, the playoffs and the Stanley Cup Final. Pekka Rinne mastered the first two, but the third had a steeper learning curve. That he was even there, though, is remarkable.

There was no NHL coverage when Rinne was growing up in Kempele, Finland, but he spent Saturday mornings watching a highlight show and modeling his game on fellow Finn Miikka Kiprusoff and Hall of Famer Dominik Hasek in the winter, while sharpening his hand-eye coordination and reaction time playing *pesapallo*, a Finnish version of baseball in the summer.

Rinne was a little known commodity when he was first eligible for the NHL entry draft in 2001. He was the backup goalie on Karpat Oulu and was passed over in his first year. And then again for two more.

In his fourth year of eligibility in 2004, the Nashville Predators drafted Rinne in the eighth round, 258th overall. The Predators only chose him because they were running out of players on their draft board and Helsinki-based scout Janne Kekalainen advocated for him. "You could easily tell he was mobile, but the most impressive thing was the energy, drive, sportsmanship oozing out of him," said Kekalainen of Rinne.

Rinne joined the American Hockey League's Milwaukee Admirals for the 2005–06 season and spent three years there before cracking the Predators' lineup full-time.

In 2008–09 the 6-foot-5, 217-pound contortionist had 29 wins, a 2.17 goals-against average and .938 save percentage to finish fourth in Calder Trophy voting.

As a testament to his consistency, after nine seasons Rinne's career goals-against average and save percentage are the exact same as his rookie year's. His playoff save percentage is also the same, and his playoff goals-against average is 0.03 lower.

Led the NHL in wins (43), saves (1,987), games (73) and points (five) in 2011–12

Voted a finalist for the Vezina Trophy three times (2011, 2012, 2015)

Won silver at the 2014 World Championship and named tournament MVP

Named to two NHL All-Star Games (2015, 2016)

The 2010–11 season was Rinne's best above this mean, with career-highs in goals-against average (2.12) and save percentage (.930). He was second in Vezina Trophy voting and fourth for the Hart Trophy.

Rinne has been a Vezina finalist three times and was named tournament MVP after winning silver at the 2014 World Championship, but the 2017 postseason was his finest hour.

Facing the Blackhawks in the opening round, Rinne stopped 59 shots over the first two games for back-to-back shutouts. He completed the sweep with an incredible .976 save percentage, including .991 in 5-on-5 play, and a 0.70 goals-against average.

After beating the St. Louis Blues in the second round, Rinne stole series-clinching Game 6 of the Western Conference Final despite the Predators being outshot 41-18 by the Anaheim Ducks. Nashville had reached the franchise's first Stanley Cup Final.

Game 1 showed that the final is a different beast, though. Entering with a .941 playoff save percent-

age, Rinne only faced 11 shots in a 5–3 loss to the Penguins for a .636 save percentage — the worst in recorded playoff history. He allowed four goals in Game 2 and was pulled in a 4–1 defeat.

Rinne couldn't stop a puck in Pittsburgh, but back in Smashville he allowed just two goals over two games as the Predators tied the series. Conn Smythe Trophy talk was revived around Rinne, until the Penguins won the series in Game 6 with a bank-shot off his back at 18:25 of the third period, which was the only goal he allowed before a Penguins empty-netter sealed the 2–0 victory.

Despite the loss his playoff magic earned him some new fans beyond Nashville, where he was already a star. "He's everyone's favorite player, including in this room too. We love him," said teammate Craig Smith. "They put the camera on him in the third or something and he makes big saves and everybody goes crazy. Everybody is on the bench doing the same thing the fans are."

TYLER SEGUIN

"Thank you, Kessel" used to be a popular refrain from fans at Boston's TD Garden whenever the Toronto Maple Leafs visited the hometown Bruins.

The genesis of the taunt was the Leafs having traded two first-round draft picks to the Bruins as part of a package for Phil Kessel, the first of which became second overall pick Tyler Seguin in 2010.

Born in 1992 in Brampton, Ontario, Seguin's hockey career took him to the elite private school St. Michael's College in Toronto, which has produced scores of NHL players since it opened in 1852. Starting at the age of 13, he woke up at 5:30 each morning so he could catch a series of buses to get to school on time.

His father, Paul, who played hockey at the University of Vermont, didn't think an easy path and continued dominance over his local peers would serve his son well down the road. "I think a lot of what was done made Tyler stronger," said Paul. "We knew there were going to be challenges in his life and in hockey. And I believe he was used to the challenges. But there were a few times when he had to have mom or dad pick up the phone or go down and see him. I think every kid needs that. But he has this amazing ability to overcome challenges, whatever they are."

At 16, Tyler traveled even farther from home, playing in Michigan for the Plymouth Whalers of the Ontario Hockey League. He scored 69 goals and 173 points in 124 games over two seasons, igniting the great Taylor/Tyler debate for the 2010 NHL entry draft. The two tied for most points in the OHL in 2009–10, with Seguin winning the Red Tilson Trophy as the OHL's Most Outstanding Player. But it was Taylor Hall who was taken first overall by the Edmonton Oilers.

Constantly being compared to Hall and Kessel and playing under coach Claude Julien, who doesn't always trust young players, Seguin endured a difficult rookie season. He averaged only eight minutes a game, and the first time he dressed in the 2011 playoffs was for Game 1 of the Eastern Conference Final.

Seguin scored a nifty goal in his playoff debut and, finally unleashed, followed it the next game with another beauty, part of a four-point period. He had three goals and seven points in 13 postseason games, as the Bruins went on to win the Stanley Cup.

"Being drafted so high in the draft, similar to Taylor Hall, you usually go to the teams that are rebuilding, to the lower place teams," said Paul. "But just because of the luck of the Kessel trade, Tyler ends up in Boston and wins a Stanley Cup."

For Toronto fans, Seguin bringing the Cup to his former home arena with the Greater Toronto Hockey League was a painful reminder of the trade. The link between Seguin and Kessel has faded, however. Kessel is now a Pittsburgh Penguin, and Seguin, after one goal and eight points in 22 playoff games, was traded just 10 days after the Bruins lost to the Blackhawks in the 2013 Cup final.

Accused of immaturity, excessive partying and not fitting into Julien's defensive system, Seguin was only 21 when the Bruins sent him to Dallas for a package that included Loui Eriksson.

In his first year in Big D, Seguin was moved to center and given more offensive freedom. He formed one of the NHL's most productive partnerships alongside Jamie Benn with 84 points in 80 games.

Over his first three seasons with the Stars, Seguin had 234 points, which was fourth best in the NHL behind only Sidney Crosby, Benn and Patrick Kane.

Seguin has also become a member of Canada's national team, winning a gold medal at the 2015 World Championship and leading all scorers with nine goals. He was named to the team again for the 2016 World Cup of Hockey but had to bow out after an injury during a pre-tournament exhibition game.

Playing with the best has helped Seguin grow into the role of an NHL star, on and off the ice. "He was like any other 21-year-old," explained Stars general manager Jim Nill of Seguin's reputation when he made the trade. "He did some things he probably would like to take back, if you could, but you learn from it.

"Tyler's probably one of the most misread guys around the league. He's infectious with people. He loves to be around them. And we're seeing him mature."

Named the OHL's Most Outstanding Player in 2010

Won the Stanley Cup in 2011

Played in four NHL All-Star Games (2012, 2015, 2016, 2017)

Won gold at the 2015 World Championship

PATRIK LAINE

For Canadians, 2016 was an *annus horribilis*. Not one Canadian team qualified for the postseason, so the most dramatic hockey coverage was the draft lottery. Five of the top six draft picks went to Canadian teams, with the Toronto Maple Leafs taking Arizona's Auston Matthews first and the Winnipeg Jets choosing Patrik Laine of Tampere, Finland, next.

Laine, for one, believed he should've been first: "I know that's how good I am, and I can say that. It's not a problem for me. And if that's a problem to somebody else, it's not my problem. I don't care what people think."

He's not wrong. Laine had already proven himself before the draft with a year for the ages.

It began with Finland winning the 2016 World Junior gold medal on home ice, with Laine scoring seven goals to share the tournament lead with Matthews. In the Finnish Elite League, Laine was first among rookies with 17 goals and 33 points in 46 games, and he led Tappara to the 2016 Finnish League championship, scoring 10 goals in 18 games to win the Jari Kurri Award as playoff MVP.

A couple weeks later Laine went to Russia for the World Championship. A boy among men — albeit a 6-foot-5, 206-pound one — he tied for the tournament lead with seven goals and was named MVP as Finland won the silver medal.

That kind of success would normally make Laine an easy choice for number one pick. Fortunately for the Jets, 2016 was not most years. Though they lost the lottery, Winnipeg was going back to the future. The first version of the team, before it moved to Arizona, had Teemu Selanne arrive from Finland and shatter the NHL rookie record with 76 goals in 1992–93. The second iteration of the Jets, formerly the Atlanta Thrashers, now had themselves a similarly electrifying Finn.

In the first eight games of his NHL career, Laine had six goals (including a hat trick), one of which featured a goal celebration that nodded to his countryman, mimicking Selanne's stick twirl before placing it back in its (imaginary) scabbard on his hip.

With his rocket of a shot and exuberant goal celebrations, Laine also brought to mind a young Alex Ovechkin — perhaps the most apt comparison for both him and Matthews.

Laine is an explosive winger, capable of blowing the puck through goaltenders, while Matthews is a more subtly skilled centerman, like Sidney Crosby. Their rivalry is also similar to Crosby and Ovechkin's, based more on proximity in age and talent and media encouragement than any real personal animosity.

Because Laine and Matthews are in different

conferences they'll have less of an opportunity to build grudges and history, which is a shame for fans. Each of the two games they faced each other in 2016–17 were thrillers, both 5–4 overtime victories for the home side. In the first, Laine had a hat trick, including the overtime winner, and he scored twice in Toronto in the second game. His second goal in Toronto was his 30th of the season, making him just the fourth player in the past two decades to score at least 30 goals in a season after being drafted. "I look back and, if I was the same age, there's no way that I'd be that ready right away," said Selanne, who was 22 when he reached the NHL. "I'm so proud of how he's played and how he's handled himself in his first season. It's unbelievable. And I know things are only going to get better for him."

For much of the season Laine was the frontrunner for the rookie scoring title and the Calder Trophy, but he missed eight games with a concussion and had a late slump. Following an 11-game stretch with 16 points, including nine goals, he went 11 games in March with only two goals and an assist. He finished 2016–17 with 36 goals and 64 points, second to Matthews in both categories and Calder voting.

Although the Jets missed the playoffs, their golden child tied for seventh in the NHL in goals, sixth in even-strength goals (27) and fourth in goals per game (0.49). Laine also played in his first All-Star Game.

After nearly a quarter-century, Winnipeg has Teemu 2.0. And that's a win.

| Won gold at the 2016 World Juniors |
| Won the Finnish Elite League championship and named playoff MVP in 2016 |
| Won silver at the 2016 World Championship and named MVP |
| Played in the 2017 NHL All-Star Game |

VLADIMIR TARASENKO

Vladimir Tarasenko scored on the first two shots of his NHL career. His grandfather was probably disappointed he didn't get the hat trick.

The goals came on January 19, 2013, against Jimmy Howard and the Detroit Red Wings, the former team of his idol Sergei Fedorov and one of the reasons Tarasenko wears number 91. It's also the year of his birth, in Novosibirsk, Siberia. Tarasenko spent much of his youth there being raised by his grandfather and namesake while his father was pursuing his own hockey dreams. Andrei Tarasenko played for 21 seasons in the Russian Superleague, winning the scoring title in 1996–97.

The elder Vladimir was the director of a soccer academy, but his grandson, whom he calls Volodya, wanted to follow in his father's skates. The young man was groomed to succeed with a little tough love from his grandparents. "When Volodya had a fever my wife would still dress him warmly and take him for a walk outside in winter. This was how we hardened him," recalled his grandfather fondly.

Tarasenko made HC Sibir Novosibirsk's second team when he was 14, scoring seven goals in one game that season. The next preseason he earned a tryout with the first team, which was coached by his father.

If there were any questions of nepotism, Tarasenko answered them by scoring a goal the first time he touched the puck in the Kontinental Hockey League.

But it wasn't always smooth sailing for father and son. "They were always punching each other, screaming at each other," said Jori Lehtera, Tarasenko's teammate on the St. Louis Blues and Novosibirsk. "They had more like a coach-player relationship."

Tarasenko eventually left his hometown to play for SKA St. Petersburg, where he was named captain at the age of 18, and after he represented Russia at the 2010 World Junior Championship, the Blues traded David Rundblad to Ottawa for the opportunity to draft him 16th overall.

In 2011 Tarasenko returned to the World Juniors as the captain of Team Russia. He left the gold medal game with a rib injury in the second period but came back for the third when Russia trailed Canada 3–0. The captain spearheaded the golden comeback with the game-tying goal and an assist on the go-ahead goal in a 5–3 win.

By 2014–15 Tarasenko had established himself as an NHL star. He led the Blues with 37 goals, which was fifth in the NHL, including one of the goals of the season under the bright lights of Broadway. He danced past four New York Rangers in Madison Square Garden and deposited the puck behind goalie Cam Talbot on the backhand with one hand, Peter Forsberg-style, then calmly celebrated with his teammates. "It wasn't a huge celebration or anything," said teammate Ryan Reaves. "He knew he'd done something pretty spectacular, everybody in the rink did, everybody in the world did. You see it all over the highlight-reel, and you hear it from everybody else, but you don't ever hear it from him."

Tarasenko finished the season with 73 points, a plus-27 rating and 264 shots. In Game 2 of the first round of playoffs, he scored his first postseason hat trick against the Minnesota Wild, half of his six goals in the six-game series.

In 2015 the Blues rewarded Tarasenko with an eight-year contract averaging $7.5 million a year, the highest in franchise history. The following season he was tops on the team with 40 goals and 74 points, and he led the Blues with nine goals as they reached the Western Conference Final.

After coming within two games of the Stanley Cup Final — and with Tarasenko gracing the cover of EA Sports' *NHL 17* — hopes and expectations were high in St. Louis for the 2016–17 season. The team underachieved, but Tarasenko reached the 30-goal plateau for the third-straight season and was the Blues' lone representative at the All-Star Game in Los Angeles. He also gave one young fan the birthday of a lifetime.

Tarasenko met Arianna Dougan, who is fighting neuroblastoma, at the Blues' Hockey Fights Cancer event in 2015. In 2017 he brought her with the team on their charter plane to Arizona and Colorado for her 11th birthday.

It's not something Tarasenko does for publicity. Teammates say he's always been shy and humble — lessons imparted by his father and grandfather.

Selected 16th overall in the 2010 NHL entry draft

Won gold at the 2011 World Junior Championship

Played in three NHL All-Star Games (2015, 2016, 2017)

Featured on the cover of EA Sports' *NHL 17*

ALEX PIETRANGELO

Alex Pietrangelo wears four rubber bands around his wrist when he plays, the colored kind that show support for a cause. There's a light-blue one for his niece, who beat kidney cancer; a dark-blue one for Liam, a 2-year-old heart transplant recipient he met in 2016; and then an orange one for Mandi Schwartz, sister of teammate Jaden Schwartz, and a blue and yellow one for Seth Lange, a St. Louis teenager, both of whom died of leukemia.

The rainbow on his wrist doesn't represent all the people he's lost. In 2001, on Pietrangelo's 11th birthday, his friend Cosmo Oppedisano succumbed to cancer. It was an early lesson of life's cruelty, in an otherwise idyllic childhood.

Pietrangelo spent his early days on a backyard rink in King City, 45 minutes north of Toronto, complete with outdoor lights, bonfires and best friends. But his talent soon outgrew his town and he joined the Toronto Junior Canadiens.

Facing the Markham Waxers, led by Steven Stamkos, at the 2005 all-Ontario bantam championship, Pietrangelo told nervous coach Tyler Cragg not to worry, just before the defenseman jumped over the boards and scored the game-winning goal. The two remained friends, and Cragg continued to train Pietrangelo well into his NHL days, until he succumbed to cancer in 2015 at the age of 44. "He always knew me as a player best," said Pietrangelo. "He watched me grow. He's always my biggest supporter too. That was the important thing."

From the Junior Canadiens, Pietrangelo was taken third overall by the Mississauga IceDogs in the 2006 Ontario Hockey League draft, two spots after Stamkos. After Pietrangelo put up 105 points over two OHL seasons, the latter season after the team moved to Niagara, the St. Louis Blues took him fourth overall in the 2008 entry draft.

The Blues pondered keeping the 18-year-old for the 2008–09 season, but he was sent back down to the OHL, where he captained the IceDogs and won a gold medal with Team Canada at the 2009 World Junior Championship. A year later he had 12 points in six World Junior games and was named the tournament's best defenseman, while adding a silver to his collection.

In his first full NHL season in 2010–11, the 6-foot-3, 205-pound defenseman showed he belonged permanently. He led all Blues defensemen in points (43), plus-minus (plus-18) and shots (161). Then at the 2011 World Championship he had five points in seven games and was voted the top defenseman.

The following season Pietrangelo led all NHL blueliners with six game-winning goals, and his 51 points were fifth among defensemen. At 22 he became the youngest defenseman in franchise history to have consecutive seasons of 40 or more points, and he finished fourth in voting for the 2012 Norris Trophy.

There was no regression in following seasons for Pietrangelo, as he became the first defenseman in franchise history to score at least 40 points in each of his first four full NHL seasons.

In 2015–16 Pietrangelo was sixth in the league in ice time, and he led the Blues to the Western Conference Final for the first time in 15 years. His 28:48 minutes of average ice time per game in the playoffs were the most by any Blues defenseman since Al MacInnis and Chris Pronger in 2001.

In the off-season Pietrangelo was named the 21st captain in team history. "He touches every facet of our team: power play, penalty kill, shutting games down, trying to score at the end of the game. He's just an elite player," explained Blues general manager Doug Armstrong. "We're certainly lucky to have him,

and when you add the character — I think he's going to be a great captain for the Blues."

Touched by tragedy off the ice, the young leader and bedrock of the Blues has gained perspective the hard way. "When you're in the moment, you try to make the best of it," said Pietrangelo. "The biggest impact it's had on me is [in appreciating] what I have. I'm healthy. My family's all healthy. There are a lot of people at any age who aren't so lucky. It's given me a whole different mindset of life."

On the ice, it's the inspiration for Pietrangelo's ultimate goal: "It makes me excited to know I could be the first captain to raise the Stanley Cup in the city of St. Louis."

Won gold at the 2009 World Junior Championship

Won silver at the 2010 World Juniors and voted best defenseman

Won gold at the 2014 Olympics

Won the 2016 World Cup of Hockey

RYAN SUTER

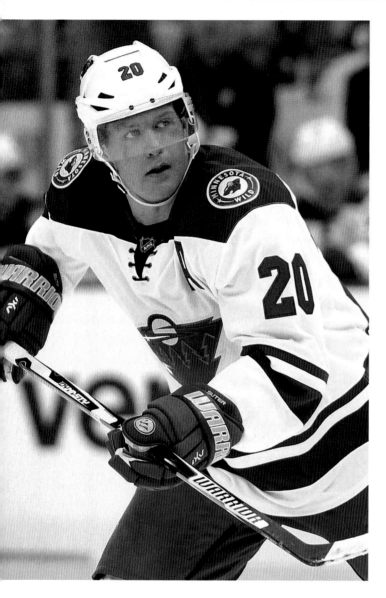

Ryan Suter is almost more impressive for what he *doesn't* do. On the ice he doesn't waste energy and rarely takes penalties; off the ice he doesn't like to draw attention to himself or his philanthropy, and he's careful with the money he's earned as a strong, silent, skilled defensemen.

Suter plays with a simplicity that's only possible because he's an intelligent player who can control the pace of the game. It also allows him to munch minutes — he's been the NHL leader in ice time three of the past four seasons.

The simplicity extends to his ride. Suter bought himself a Ford SUV with his rookie contract and drove it for 11 years, until his wife encouraged him to upgrade to a Cadillac Escalade. "I feel guilty driving that car," said Suter, "because my dad never had that."

Ryan wears number 20 as a tribute to his father, Bob, who was a member of the 1980 U.S. Olympic hockey team that upset the Soviet Union in the Miracle on Ice. Bob was drafted by the Los Angeles Kings but never played in the NHL. After his minor league career ended he opened a sporting goods store and ran the Madison Capitols youth hockey organization that Ryan's grandfather co-founded.

After his son was drafted by the Nashville Predators seventh overall in 2003 Bob would drive nine hours to watch him play and then drive right back after the game to open Bob Suter's Capitol Ice Arena in Middleton, Wisconsin. He died of a heart attack there in 2014. Ryan's younger brother now runs the arena and coaches the under-18 team, and his mother works in hockey administration. In the off-season Ryan practices with the kids and helps with arena renovations. "They're hockey royalty here," said Tom Garrity, manager of the Tier 1 Capitols.

Like his uncle, Gary Suter, who won the 1986 Calder Trophy and the 1989 Stanley Cup, Ryan has also become NHL royalty.

After a post-draft season at the University of Wisconsin and one with the Milwaukee Admirals of the American Hockey League, Suter joined the Predators in 2004–05 and had an assist on Nashville's first goal of the season.

In 2006–07 he was paired with fellow 2003 draftee Shea Weber, and over the next six seasons they were arguably the best blue line tandem in the NHL. Through 2011–12, Suter was 14th among NHL defensemen with 185 assists, Weber led all defensemen with 97 goals and the Predators made the playoffs five times.

The pair broke up in 2012, when Suter took his talents to Minnesota. There he signed a 13-year, $98 million free agent contract with the Wild, as did

Zach Parise, one of Suter's best friends and a team-mate on the U.S. team that won silver at the 2010 Olympics. Leaving Nashville was difficult, but Suter's wife grew up in the Twin Cities and Minnesota was the closest team to his family.

In his first season with the Wild, Suter was a First Team All-Star and the runner up for the Norris Trophy after averaging almost 29:24 minutes a game, which was 2:20 more than anyone else in the league. He was the first player since Nicklas Lidstrom in 2002–03 to surpass the 29-minute mark.

Won gold at the 2004 World Junior Championship

Won silver at the 2010 Olympics

Played in three NHL All-Star Games (2012, 2015, 2017)

Led the NHL in average ice time in 2012–13, 2013–14 and 2014–15

A believer in rolling six defensemen, new coach Bruce Boudreau limited his minutes in 2016–17, but Suter still tied for the league lead with a plus-34 rating, playing all 82 games with only 34 penalty minutes.

The 2017 playoffs forced a change in philosophy, however, as Boudreau leaned on his most steady and reliable player. In a 2–1 loss to the St. Louis Blues in a first round game, Suter played 34:32 minutes and the Wild outshot the Blues 52-26. When Suter was on the ice they had a 26-4 advantage in shots, when he wasn't it was 26-22. "He never gets upset, never wavers," said Wild goalie Devan Dubnyk. "He's just an absolute rock back there."

The Wild lost the series in five games, with Suter averaging over 29 minutes a game. It was the kind of workmanlike effort his dad would have been proud of, and when it was over Suter was back in Wisconsin, helping out at his father's namesake arena.

DEVAN DUBNYK

What a difference a year makes. In 12 months Devan Dubnyk went from languishing in the American Hockey League and asking to be released to being a Vezina Trophy finalist.

In 2004 the Regina, Saskatchewan, native was named the Canadian Hockey League's Scholastic Player of the Year and was taken 14th overall by the Edmonton Oilers in the entry draft. Calm, funny and smart, the 6-foot-6 Dubnyk had the necessary qualities for success in an NHL crease. He would need them all to take the slings and arrows of the profession.

After being drafted Dubnyk spent two more seasons in junior with the Kamloops Blazers, then a year with the Stockton Thunder in the East Coast Hockey League and finally two and a half seasons with the American Hockey League's Springfield Falcons. He finally stuck with the Oilers in 2010–11. "As a young player you have no idea what it's going to take. And that's probably a good thing, because it's pretty daunting," said Dubnyk. "I was called up 11 times, up and down, from Springfield. Like all young goalies, I thought I could get [to the NHL] fast but it's really so rare."

Between 2010 and 2013 Dubnyk had a .917 save percentage and 2.58 goals-against average. However, over 32 games in the final year of his contract in 2013–14, his goals-against average ballooned to 3.36 while his save percentage dropped to .894. Disgruntled Edmonton fans and the media weren't shy in expressing their derision.

Management shipped him to the Nashville Predators in January 2014, and in his only two games with the Predators, Dubnyk allowed nine goals. He was then traded to the Montreal Canadiens and played eight games the rest of the season, all with the AHL's Hamilton Bulldogs. "That's falling a long way," said Dubnyk's agent and former NHL goalie Mike Liut. "He wasn't even the starter in Hamilton. He was part of a three-man rotation. Goaltenders have bad seasons. I had bad seasons. Devan was going through as tough a time as anybody I've represented."

Dubnyk was miserable and a long way from his wife, Jennifer, and their newborn son, Nathaniel, who were back in Edmonton. Even after Carey Price got hurt in the 2014 playoffs he was still third on the depth chart behind Dustin Tokarski and Peter Budaj, so Dubnyk asked to leave the team to be with his family. "I was in no situation, either where my game was or mentally, to be playing in the playoffs for the Montreal Canadiens," said Dubnyk.

Returning home was the reset he needed. He still believed he could play and the Arizona Coyotes agreed, signing him to a one-year, $800,000 deal. Both Dubnyk's technique and confidence improved under Arizona goalie coach Sean Burke, and as Mike Smith's backup he put up decent numbers in 19 games.

On January 15, 2015, exactly one year after Edmonton traded him, the desperate Minnesota Wild acquired Dubnyk. They were 18-19-5 and eight points out of a playoff spot. "To be as honest as possible, we were just trying to get a save," according to Wild general manager Chuck Fletcher. "We were losing a lot of games, and our season was right on the brink of getting away from us. We got very lucky. Good fortune smiled warmly upon us."

Dubnyk shut out the Buffalo Sabres and started the next 38 games. With their new goalie in net the Wild went an incredible 27-9-2 with Dubnyk posting a 1.72 goals-against average and a .936 save percentage. He was a finalist for the Vezina Trophy, finished fourth in voting for the Hart and won the 2015 Masterton Trophy for perseverance, sportsmanship and dedication to hockey.

In 2017, heading into his second consecutive All-Star Game, Dubnyk's .936 save percentage and 1.88 goals-against average were tops in the NHL. After a bit of a slump he finished the season tied for seventh in save percentage (.923) and eighth in goals-against average (2.25). "When things don't go well, you can feel sorry for yourself or you can stick with it," related Smith. "He came to Arizona with a great attitude, and now he's playing the best hockey of his life in Minnesota, and he's one of the top goaltenders in the league. You hope to rub off on a guy in a good way, but he worked real hard, and I'm really proud of him. He deserves to be where he is today."

Named WHL and CHL Scholastic Player of the Year in 2004

Won gold at the 2006 World Junior Championship

Awarded the Bill Masterton Trophy in 2015

Ranked top 10 in wins, goals-against average, save percentage and shutouts in 2014–15 and 2016–17

Played in two NHL All-Star Games (2016, 2017)

NATHAN MacKINNON

CENTRAL DIVISION | Avalanche | Center

The town of Cole Harbour, Nova Scotia, has about 25,000 residents and probably the highest quotient of hockey talent per capita on the planet. Not only did the town produce Sidney Crosby, one of the top players to ever grace NHL ice, but it also gave the world Nathan MacKinnon.

MacKinnon put skates on at just 2 years old. His father, Graham, a former goalie, set up the garage as a "shooting gallery," according to his mom, Kathy. "He wouldn't put the pads on — his knees are too bad for that," said Nathan, recalling his games with his dad. "But he'd get in there and use his feet to stop my shots when I was little. But then I learned how to lift it and he couldn't play net anymore."

As he did with his father's aged goaltending skills,

MacKinnon quickly outgrew the local hockey scene. Still just 14, he left Cole Harbour to attend Shattuck-St. Mary's, the same school that Crosby played for.

After two years at boarding school MacKinnon came home to play for the Quebec Major Junior Hockey League's Halifax Mooseheads, about 10 miles west of Cole Harbour. "We had it in our heads that when he went to Shattuck, he probably wouldn't ever be home again," said Kathy. "I had convinced myself then that I had to get used to it. But when it came to be that he'd be playing in Halifax, that was a real treat."

MacKinnon led the Mooseheads to their first Memorial Cup in 2013, scoring seven goals and six assists in four games to take home the Stafford Smythe Memorial Trophy as tournament MVP.

Another Cole Harbour quality is the ability to rise to the occasion. Against the Portland Winterhawks and Seth Jones, the top-ranked skater in the upcoming entry draft, MacKinnon had a hat trick in a win in the preliminary round. Facing them again in the final, he had another hat trick, including an empty-netter to clinch the title.

Jones ended up going fourth to the Nashville Predators. The Colorado Avalanche picked MacKinnon first overall in the 2013 entry draft.

MacKinnon made his Avalanche debut at 18 years and 31 days old, making him the youngest player in franchise history. In his first game he had two assists in a 6–1 victory over the Anaheim Ducks, and he finished the 2013–14 season leading all rookies in assists (39) and points (63) and tied for the most goals (24). He capped it off by becoming the youngest player (at 18 years and 224 days old) to win the Calder Trophy as rookie of the year in 2014.

With Hall of Famer Patrick Roy behind the bench the Avalanche had a stunning turnaround with

MacKinnon in the lineup and won the division. He had three assists in Game 1 of the first round against the Minnesota Wild to become the first rookie in history with three points in his playoff debut.

The season would be the high water mark in Denver, however. The Avalanche missed the next two playoffs, and Roy quit as coach in 2016. MacKinnon led the last place Avalanche in scoring in 2016–17 and was Colorado's only representative at the 2017 All-Star Game.

The label of first overall, the Crosby connection and a seven-year, $44.1 million contract all add up to a heavy burden for a kid who is only 22 at the start of his fifth NHL season in 2017–18. And lot of the tension comes from within. "I put a lot of pressure on myself and I always have," said MacKinnon. "Hopefully this is just a down year. I feel like I handle pressure well. I play my best in the big games."

Though there weren't many big NHL games for

MacKinnon in 2016–17 he did have a few as a member of Team North America at the 2016 World Cup of Hockey. The 23-and-under team was a fan favorite with its mix of speed, skill and the fearlessness of youth.

Team North America didn't advance in the tournament but its final game was a victory over Team Sweden. MacKinnon won it in overtime with a nifty deke on New York Rangers legend Henrik Lundqvist, which he celebrated with unbridled joy. "I saw his stick came up for a poke check and managed to beat that and get it up," recounted MacKinnon. "It was fun, a fun goal."

Named Memorial Cup MVP in 2013

Selected first overall in the 2013 NHL entry draft

Won the 2014 Calder Trophy, the youngest player ever to win it

Played in the 2017 NHL All-Star Game

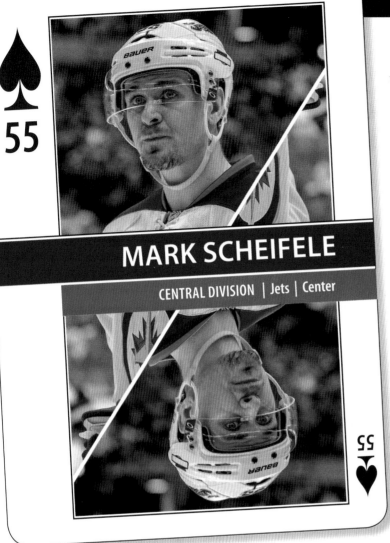

MARK SCHEIFELE

CENTRAL DIVISION | Jets | Center

Mark Scheifele is a hockey nerd. Although he's tired of the label, it fits, and it's the reason he's climbed the NHL ladder.

Growing up in Kitchener, Ontario, Scheifele was a sports obsessive. "He would sit in this big white chair in the living room, eating his cereal as he was watching SportsCentre," said his father, Brad.

All three Scheifele kids played sports, but Mark was the most serious and the most competitive. "I was always the worst loser," he recalled. "Anytime I lost it was a big ordeal ... I just couldn't stand for losing."

The drive was inborn, not taught. The Scheifele parents insisted their children play multiple sports and have fun in each of them. Mark played hockey, soccer, lacrosse, volleyball and track and field, and he left a

trail of broken equipment when things didn't go his way. Never his precious hockey sticks, though — they were too valuable.

Scheifele didn't focus on hockey until he was 16. He was chosen in the seventh round by the Saginaw Spirit in 2009 but was sent home after training camp.

Back in Kitchener with the Junior B Dutchmen, Scheifele had 55 points in 51 games and was the league's rookie of the year. Scheifele's OHL rights were then acquired by the Barrie Colts, where coach Dale Hawerchuk — Winnipeg's first-overall draft pick in 1981, a former Jets captain and a Hall of Fame inductee — convinced him to learn and grow under his tutelage.

The Colts finished last in the OHL in 2010–11, but Scheifele had 75 points in 66 games and climbed into the low first round in NHL draft rankings. A few eyebrows were raised when the Jets picked him seventh overall in 2011, their first selection after the franchise had relocated from Atlanta. "When it happened, it just felt so surreal," recalled Brad Scheifele. "I was so overwhelmed by the whole thing. We all were."

Winnipeg scouts Marcel Comeau and Mark Hillier went out on a limb for Scheifele. Management knew he wasn't going to stroll right into the NHL as an 18-year-old, but they believed he had the work ethic to get there and the humility to realize he'd need it.

Scheifele's first NHL game was also the reborn Jets' first since returning to Manitoba, and his first goal came four games later, in front of family in Toronto, against the Maple Leafs on October 19, 2011. It was his only point in 11 regular-season games with the Jets over his first two seasons; the rest were back in Barrie, where he had 142 points in 92 combined games.

Only 175 pounds when drafted, Scheifele knew he had to change his body to become an NHL regular, so in 2013 he sought out Gary Roberts, the fitness guru

to many of the league's stars. Roberts trained Scheifele six days a week in the summer and tailored a nutrition program based on his DNA, building him into a prototypical power forward at 6-foot-3 and 207 pounds.

In 2013–14 Scheifele stuck with the team permanently and slowly moved up the depth chart at center over the next two seasons. Then in early 2016, after inheriting the first line role, Scheifele showed what he was truly capable of. In 82 games between January 2016 and January 2017, his 85 points trailed only Sidney Crosby and Connor McDavid.

Scheifele played on Team North America's top line at the 2016 World Cup of Hockey with McDavid and Auston Matthews, the first overall draft picks in 2015 and 2016, respectively. The immediate success of these two teenagers was a contrast to 23-year-old Scheifele's comparatively long road to stardom.

Jets rookie Patrik Laine was another example of an instant star. The second overall pick in 2016

and Scheifele's winger represented Winnipeg at the 2017 All-Star Game, leaving Scheifele as the only player among the top 10 scorers who wasn't in the game. Scheifele finished 2016–17 with 32 goals and 82 points, 21 more than his previous career high and good for seventh in the league.

Not all NHL stars are born. Some are created with time and utter devotion to the game. "I don't think there could ever be a day in my life where hockey's not a part of it," said Scheifele. "I literally live and breathe hockey and it's the love of my life."

Spoken like a true nerd.

Selected seventh overall in the 2011 NHL entry draft

Won bronze at the 2012 World Juniors

Finished seventh in NHL scoring with 82 points in 2016–17

Won the 2016 World Championship

♠
33

DUSTIN BYFUGLIEN

CENTRAL DIVISION | Jets | Defense

33
♠

Whether he's filling out a uniform or a stat sheet, Big Buff is hard to miss. Officially listed at 6-foot-5 and 260 pounds, give or take a little on the weight, Dustin Byfuglien is a wrecking ball. But it's not just hits and penalty minutes. He's also racking up ice time, shots, goals and assists. Not that he's checking out the box scores the next day. Sports, according to Byfuglien, "aren't my cup of tea."

That might be the reason for Byfuglien's laissez-faire attitude toward hockey growing up, and even after his name was called at the NHL entry draft.

Byfuglien spent his childhood in Roseau, Minnesota, living in a trailer with his mother in her parents' yard. He was good enough to make the Roseau Rams, winners of seven state high school championships, but his grades weren't up to standard so he just practiced with the team. "I was like, 'Whatever, I'll just go do something different. I'll go fishing, I'll go snowmobiling,'" recalled Byfuglien.

Word spread about the linebacker in skates anyway, and the Chicago Mission midget team invited Byfuglien to join them. "I think that's when I realized that, alright, I can actually, probably, maybe, do something, a little bit, with this hockey stuff," he said.

Byfuglien was taken by the Brandon Wheat Kings in the seventh round of the 2001 Western Hockey League draft then was later traded to the Prince George Cougars. In 2002–03, his NHL draft season, he had 39 points in 56 games, nine more points than fellow WHL defenseman Dion Phaneuf in 15 fewer games.

While Phaneuf was selected ninth overall in 2003, Byfuglien had to wait until the eighth round, 245th overall, for the Chicago Blackhawks to call his name. Not that he was aware of it. The Blackhawks couldn't reach him after the draft and finally had to show up at the family home to inform him. "Normally when they get that call, it's the happiest day, the biggest day in a kid's life," recounted general manager Stan Bowman. "Buff didn't even know he'd been drafted."

Byfuglien, who'd been up to 280 pounds in junior, "probably came into the league as the rawest player in the game" according to then-Blackhawks teammate Brian Campbell. But he made it because "he's an athlete. He may not look like it, but he is."

Byfuglien's first full season was in 2007–08, which included a move from defense to forward. He's switched back and forth throughout his career when the need has arisen, evidence of his underrated skating ability and high hockey IQ.

Byfuglien spent most of the 2009–10 season on defense, but moved up to forward for the playoffs. He tied for the team lead with 11 playoff goals, including a hat trick in the second round against the Vancouver Canucks, three game-winners in a sweep of the San Jose Sharks in the Western Conference Final, a two-goal, four-point night in Game 5 of the Stanley Cup Final against the Philadelphia Flyers and a goal in the Game 6 win that clinched Chicago's first Cup in 49 years. That was his swansong in Chicago, however. Hard against the salary cap, the Blackhawks traded him to Atlanta during the summer.

Playing defense for the Thrashers in 2010–11,

Byfuglien's 20 goals and 53 points ranked first and fourth among all NHL defenseman, and he played in his first All-Star Game. For the 2011–12 season, after one year in Atlanta, he relocated with the team to Winnipeg. Byfuglien has since played in three more All-Star Games.

Now an elder statesman on the NHL's second-youngest team, Byfuglien sets an example with his energy and effort. He led the league in average ice time in 2016–17 (27:26), and among defensemen he was fifth in points (52), second in shots (241) and second in penalty minutes (117).

He's also become a trusted voice to the coaches and management, picking up nuances of games and players. Just don't ask the hockey savant to get too in-depth.

When the media inquired how the Jets won their last seven games of the 2016–17 season, Byfuglien replied, "(We) outscored our opponents." Big Buff likes to keep it simple.

Won the Stanley Cup in 2010

Played in four NHL All-Star Games (2011, 2012, 2015, 2016)

Led the NHL in average ice time in 2016–17 (27:26)

Played for Team USA at the 2016 World Cup of Hockey

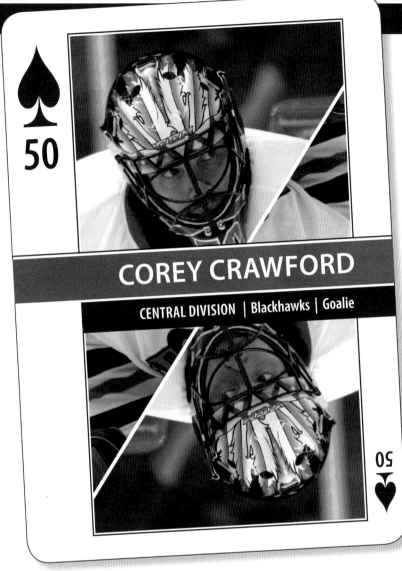

♠

50

COREY CRAWFORD

CENTRAL DIVISION | Blackhawks | Goalie

50
♠

It's a good time to be a Blackhawk. After years of irrelevance, the Original Six team won three Stanley Cups in six years, from 2010 to 2015, after a 49-year drought, and it has superstars at every position. Even at goaltender.

Forwards Patrick Kane and Jonathan Toews and defenseman Duncan Keith need no introduction. Between them they've won four Olympic gold medals, three Conn Smythes, two Norris Trophies, a Ted Lindsay Award, a Hart, an Art Ross, a Calder and a Selke.

And then there's Corey Crawford, stopping pucks under those enormous shadows.

Growing up on Montreal's South Shore in Châteauguay, Quebec, Crawford idolized the Canadiens' Patrick Roy and wore his No. 33 at Howard S. Billings High School.

The two goalies couldn't have had more disparate career paths, though. Roy won the Stanley Cup and Conn Smythe Trophy as a 20-year-old in his rookie season, and the brash, outspoken winner of three more Cups and three Vezinas is considered by some as the greatest goaltender of all time.

Crawford, on the other hand, "wasn't someone you saw and immediately thought he was going to be an NHL superstar," according to Frantz Jean, Crawford's goalie coach with the Moncton Wildcats, who drafted him 14th overall in the 2001 Quebec Major Junior Hockey League draft. But the tall, gangly goalie made enough of an impression on the Blackhawks to be drafted in the second round, 52nd overall, in 2003. In his first American Hockey League season, Crawford's goals-against average was almost 3.00 and his save percentage was a shade under .900. Those numbers don't get you called up, but he added weight and strength and worked on his stickhandling to add to his solid fundamentals. "We told him he would have to work, and he did, but just like in the NHL, it didn't always come easy," said Mike Haviland, who coached Crawford in the AHL and NHL.

Crawford made his NHL debut on January 22, 2006, but he spent the majority of five seasons in the minors. When the Blackhawks won the Stanley Cup in 2010, Crawford was in the AHL. He earned a regular spot in 2010–11 in which he had a 176:09 shutout streak and tied a Blackhawks rookie record with eight straight wins.

In 2012–13, Crawford and Ray Emery combined to win the Jennings Trophy for allowing the fewest goals in the NHL. Crawford was third in the NHL with a 1.94 goals-against average, and lowered it to

1.84 with a .932 save percentage in the playoffs as Chicago won the 2013 Stanley Cup.

And captain Jonathan Toews credited Crawford for his second Cup: "Patrick Kane won the Conn Smythe, but if we had our choice, for sure it would have been [Crawford]."

Two years later Crawford added his second Jennings Trophy (sharing it with Carey Price of the Montreal Canadiens), played in his first NHL All-Star Game and won his second Stanley Cup. With the Blackhawks trailing the Tampa Bay Lightning two games to one in the 2015 Cup final, he allowed just two goals over the last three games.

In 2015–16 Crawford led the NHL with seven shutouts, including three in a four-game stretch — the first Blackhawks goalie to do that since Tony Esposito in 1974. Yet he was passed over for the All-Star Game.

Asked if that bothered him, Crawford replied, "No. It is what it is. It would've been nice to go, but to take a little time off is always nice, too."

Crawford doesn't care if people think he is riding his teammates' coattails or that his success is because of the team in front of him: "People can argue one way and others can argue another — that's just chatter. I just play hard and if you have the respect of your teammates and if your fans are on your side that's all that matters."

After backing up Price and winning the title at the 2016 World Cup of Hockey, Crawford had his sixth-straight full season with at least 30 wins, and he played in his second All-Star Game in 2017. Joining him were Kane, Toews and Keith, of course.

Named to the 2011 NHL All-Rookie Team
Won the Stanley Cup twice (2013, 2015)
Won the William Jennings Trophy twice (2013, 2015)
Played in two NHL All-Star Games (2015, 2017)
Won the 2016 World Cup of Hockey

MARIAN HOSSA

CENTRAL DIVISION | Blackhawks | Right Wing | 81

- Selected 12th overall in the 1997 NHL entry draft
- Won the WHL title and Memorial Cup in 1998
- Was an NHL All-Rookie Team selection in 1998–99
- Played in five NHL All-Star Games (2001, 2003, 2007, 2008, 2012)
- Named Slovakian Player of the Year in 2007, 2008, 2009 and 2012
- Won the Stanley Cup three times (2010, 2013, 2015)
- Runner up at the 2016 World Cup of Hockey

For a while Marian Hossa couldn't win for losing. Accustomed to success — he had won the Slovak Extraliga title at 17 with HC Dukla Trencin and the Western Hockey League championship and Memorial Cup with the Portland Winter Hawks when he was 19 — the Stanley Cup proved difficult to win, especially when he got tantalizingly close.

Born in Stara Lubovna, Czechoslovakia (now Slovakia), Hossa was drafted 12th overall by the Senators in 1997 and went on to score 30 or more goals four times with Ottawa, including 45 in 2002–03 when the Senators reached Game 7 of the Eastern Conference Final.

Prior to the 2005–06 season, the Senators and Atlanta Thrashers flipped young superstars, with Dany Heatley going to Ottawa. In Atlanta Hossa was getting further away from hockey's Holy Grail with the moribund Thrashers, until he was dealt in 2008 to the star-laden Pittsburgh Penguins at the trade deadline. The Penguins reached the Stanley Cup Final but fell to the Detroit Red Wings in six games.

A free agent at the end of the season, Hossa turned down an $80 million offer from the Edmonton Oilers for a one-year deal with the Red Wings in pursuit of the Cup. In 2008–09 with Detroit he became the eighth player to score 40 goals with three different teams, but he backed the wrong horse. Pittsburgh got its revenge by beating the Wings in seven games in a Stanley Cup Final rematch.

A free agent once again Hossa found a home and a winner with the Chicago Blackhawks. In 2010 he became the first player to appear in three Stanley Cup Finals with three different teams, and this time he was on the winning side.

The Blackhawks captured the Cup again in 2013 and 2015, and Hossa started racking up his own personal accomplishments.

Playing his 1,100th NHL game back in Ottawa on October 30, 2014, Hossa had a goal and an assist to become the 80th player in NHL history to reach 1,000 points. And two years later, on October 18, 2016, against the Philadelphia Flyers, he became the 44th member of the NHL's 500-goal club.

After scoring 188 goals for the Senators, 108 with the Thrashers, 40 with the Red Wings and three with the Penguins, Hossa's 161st goal for Chicago made him the fifth player to reach 500 while in a Blackhawks uniform, after Bobby Hull, Stan Mikita, Michel Goulet and Peter Bondra.

A few weeks later Hossa scored his 504th to pass Bondra for the most NHL goals by a Slovakian. He finished the 2016–17 season with 525, fourth among active players behind Jaromir Jagr (765), Jarome Iginla (625) and Alex Ovechkin (558). With 1,134 career points Hossa is also fourth on the active list behind Jagr (1,914), Joe Thornton (1,391) and Iginla (1,300), third in even-strength goals (348) and fifth in game-winning goals (85).

All told it took 12 seasons for Hossa to capture his first Stanley Cup. He has experienced a similar drought in international play, where he's still looking for his first championship. He came close at the 2016 World Cup of Hockey as part of Team Europe, which was runner-up to Team Canada.

At 6-foot-1 and 207 pounds, with speed and strength, Hossa plays both ends of the ice and every part of the game. He's led the NHL in shorthanded goals twice and is the active career leader with 34, while being fifth in power-play goals with 143.

For almost two decades Hossa has been one of the NHL's most versatile players and reliable scorers, but on teams with forwards like Crosby and Malkin, Datsyuk and Zetterberg, Toews and Kane, he hasn't always received his due. His stats, however, are undeniable, and his teammates have no doubt that he belongs with the best, on the ice and off. "He's one of those players when I was a kid that you looked up to and idolized and would really be wowed by his presence on the ice," said former Chicago teammate Kris Versteeg, who won two Cups with Hossa. "He's a special guy. He takes time to consider other people. He could be the ultimate All-Star and never talk to anyone, but he talks to everyone and really gets to know everybody. He's honestly the best team guy and All-Star I've ever played with."

PACIFIC DIVISION

FIRST STARS

SECOND STARS

BLACK ACES

MILESTONES

RYAN GETZLAF

Won gold at the 2005 World Junior Championship

Won the Stanley Cup in 2007

Won gold at the 2010 and 2014 Olympics

Named captain of the Anaheim Ducks in 2010

Won the 2016 World Cup of Hockey

The Mark Messier NHL Leadership Award is given "to the player who exemplifies great leadership qualities to his team, on and off the ice during the regular season."

It's an apt comparison for 2017 finalist Ryan Getzlaf. Like Messier, the Anaheim Ducks captain is a physical presence who will drop his gloves to help his team, but he's just as likely to change the course of a game with his soft hands and playmaking. "He has a bad temper, a high skill level and a big body," said former Ducks general manager Brian Burke. "That's a good combination for a hockey player."

The 6-foot-4, 221-pound center had amassed 578 assists in his career by the end of the 2016–17 season, more than 70 percent of his 814 total points, as well as 730 penalty minutes.

Getzlaf was born in Regina, Saskatchewan, where he started skating when he was just 3 years old and playing competitively at 5. It wasn't all hockey in the household, though. He was a provincial champion in baseball and his brother, Chris, grew up to be a slotback in the Canadian Football League.

When Getzlaf was selected in the third round of the 2000 Western Hockey League draft by the Calgary Hitmen he was 5-foot-10. Halfway through his rookie season he was 6-foot-2. After watching him rack up points and penalty minutes in the WHL, the Ducks drafted Getzlaf 19th overall in 2003.

Two years later, with the NHL in a lockout, Canada put together what's generally acknowledged as its most talented World Junior roster in history. Getzlaf led that 2005 team with nine assists in six games and was second with 12 points, one behind Patrice Bergeron, as they took home the gold.

Getzlaf's first full NHL season came in 2006–07, and in the playoffs he had 17 points to help the Ducks win their first Stanley Cup. He followed that up with an 82-point season, and in 2008–09 he had a career-high 91 points and set a Ducks single-season record with 66 assists.

In 2010 Getzlaf won his first Olympic gold, with

three goals and seven points, and was named captain of the Ducks. In 2014 he won another gold medal at the Sochi Games and finished second in Hart Trophy voting after getting 87 points, which included a career-best 31 goals. Two years later he won the title at the 2016 World Cup of Hockey.

In 2016–17 Getzlaf had 73 points, and his 58 assists were third in the NHL, as he passed Teemu Selanne for the most career assists in Ducks history. Over the last six weeks of the season he had 27 points in 18 games, led all NHL forwards in shifts per game and was second in average ice time in that span.

In the second round Getzlaf showed Edmonton's Connor McDavid how it's done in the playoffs. In Game 4 Getzlaf had four points, the last one after blocking a shot then going down the ice to set up Jakob Silfverberg for the 4–3 overtime winner. In Game 5 his goal sparked a three-goal comeback in the final 3:16 of regulation time before he assisted

on the double-OT winner. Powered by their captain, the Ducks won the series in seven to make it to the Western Conference Final, where they eventually fell to the Nashville Predators. In 17 playoff games Getzlaf had 19 points, which was the most in the conference and second in the NHL when the Ducks were eliminated.

Getzlaf's leadership qualities extend off the ice as well. He has a cousin with autism, which had a profound effect on him and sent him on a philanthropic path. After playing for the Hitmen Getzlaf started a foundation for underprivileged youth in Calgary, and he raises funds for Duchenne muscular dystrophy. It's a cause that touched him deeply after he met Hawken Miller, a young man in Anaheim who lives with DMD.

Both on and off the ice Getzlaf has evolved into one of the league's most recognized leaders. Over the course of his distinguished career his body of work and his hairline are positively Messier-esque.

ANZE KOPITAR

One of the most coveted assets in hockey is a big, offensively gifted yet defensively responsible centerman. To find such a unicorn, the Los Angeles Kings went all the way to Slovenia, a country of two million people that has just seven rinks and about 150 registered senior men's players.

Anze Kopitar, from Jesenice, a town in the northern part of the country near the Austrian border, is the first Slovene to play in the NHL.

More common is his origin story. Playing on a backyard rink that his grandfather flooded, Anze spent hours out there pretending to be his dad, Matjaz, who was a national team player.

"He was always scoring big goals in big games, so I always wanted to be that guy, too," said Anze. "He was in the national championship, and I thought that was the best thing."

It was the biggest stage he could imagine as a boy, but when Slovenia hosted an international tournament, scouts who came to see players from the usual European hockey powers discovered a local product who could play. In 2004, at the age of 16, Kopitar left to play for Sodertalje SK in Sweden.

In 2005 Kopitar had 10 goals and 13 points for Slovenia in the B pool of the World Junior Championship, and 11 points in five games at the Under-18 tournament. He also represented his country at the highest level for the first time in Olympic qualifying and at the World Championship, with his father as assistant coach.

It was the same year the Kings picked him 11th overall in the entry draft, and Kopitar made his NHL debut at 19 years old on October 6, 2006, scoring two goals against the Anaheim Ducks. In his second game he had three assists against the St. Louis Blues.

Kopitar led the Kings in scoring in 2007–08, the start of nine straight seasons that the center ranked first on the team. With 74 points in 2015–16 he broke Marcel Dionne's franchise record of eight consecutive years (1975–76 to 1982–83).

By the end of the 2016–17 season Kopitar had accumulated 736 points in 840 games, and 64 points in 75 playoff games. The latter included eight goals and 20 points in the 2012 playoffs, tied with then-captain Dustin Brown atop the NHL, to help lead the Kings to the franchise's first Stanley Cup.

In 2014 Wayne Gretzky, who knows a thing about playing in LA and being great, called Kopitar the third-best player in the world, behind Jonathan Toews and Sidney Crosby. In the playoffs, he bettered them both, leading all players in assists (21) and points (26) as the Kings won their second championship.

Earlier in 2014 Slovenia defied all odds and logic by reaching the quarterfinals of the Sochi Olympics. At the helm was Matjaz Kopitar, who was cut from the Yugoslavian team just before the Sarajevo Olympics in 1984 but 30 years later fulfilled his Olympic dream as head coach of Slovenia. Anze was the only NHL player on the Slovenian Olympic team.

The 2015–16 season was a banner one for Kopitar, who won the Frank J. Selke Trophy as best defensive forward and the Lady Byng Trophy for being the league's most sportsmanlike player. The Kings rewarded him with an eight-year, $80 million contract in 2016. It made him the third-highest paid player in the NHL, after Patrick Kane and Toews, but the highest in 2016–17 with the front-loaded deal.

In September 2016 he captained Team Europe at the World Cup of Hockey. It was the second team that named him captain that summer after the Kings took the C off Brown's jersey and gave it to Kopitar, who had been Brown's lieutenant and alternate for eight seasons. "It's time for Kopitar to take over," explained Dean Lombardi, Kings president and general manager at the time. "He's one of our best players, and he's moving into his prime. It's his turn."

"Bottom line, guys like Kopitar, their best years are in front of [them]. Guys get rewarded for winning Stanley Cups," said Darryl Sutter, the Kings coach at the time. "You win championships with players like that, very clear; he's worth every penny."

Mike Futa, Los Angeles' director of hockey operations and director of player personnel, agreed: "He's everything we covet as a King. Anytime we write out our core and what has made us successful, the first name we write down is our C1, number 11."

Played in the NHL YoungStars Game in 2007

Played in three NHL All-Star Games (2008, 2011, 2015)

Won the Stanley Cup twice (2012, 2014)

Received the Frank J. Selke and Lady Byng Trophies in 2016

Named captain of the Los Angeles Kings in 2016

CONNOR McDAVID

In 2015 Edmonton officially stopped calling itself the City of Champions. Posted on signs entering the city, the slogan celebrated the community's response to a 1987 tornado and the hockey team that was in the midst of winning five Stanley Cups. City councilors might have been premature in voting to remove them, however. In 2015 the Oilers drafted the most hyped and anticipated player since Sidney Crosby.

Growing up in Newmarket, Ontario, Connor McDavid always played with older kids and his York Simcoe Express team won provincial championships in novice, minor atom, atom, minor peewee and peewee. With a relentless internal drive and a mind for the game, he left to attend the Premier Elite Athletes' Collegiate in Toronto. There he proved he didn't have just hockey intellect; he also moved up a year academically.

At 15 McDavid became the third player ever to be granted Exceptional Player Status to join the Ontario Hockey League a year early. The Erie Otters took him first overall, and McDavid won back-to-back OHL and Canadian Hockey League Scholastic Player of the Year awards in 2014 and 2015.

In 2014–15 McDavid won both the OHL and CHL Player of the Year honors, despite missing six weeks with a broken hand. The injury caused a national crisis when it appeared he might not play in the World Juniors, but his cast came off days before it started and he had a tournament-leading eight assists in seven games as Canada won the gold.

McDavid finished the OHL season with 44 goals, 120 points and a plus-60 rating in only 47 games, and added 49 points in 20 playoff games as the Otters lost to the Oshawa Generals in the OHL final.

Crosby was McDavid's idol, and once McDavid hit the NHL he proved he was Crosby's heir apparent, perhaps even his superior. Crosby admits the 6-foot-1, 200-pound center is "far and away the fastest guy I've seen," which was proven when McDavid broke the 21-year-old record for fastest skater at the 2017 All-Star Game skills competition.

Named OHL and CHL Scholastic Player of the Year in 2014 and 2015

Named the OHL's Most Outstanding Player and CHL Player of the Year in 2015

Won gold at the 2015 World Juniors

Won gold at the 2016 World Championship

Won the Art Ross and Hart Trophies in 2017

His breathtaking speed is one of the reasons McDavid missed almost half of his rookie season in 2015–16. He was about to blow by two Philadelphia Flyers defenders in a November game when he was taken down hard and clumsily. Flying full speed into the end boards, he broke his collarbone and missed 37 games. He still finished third in Calder Trophy voting after getting 48 points in 45 games.

Prior to the 2016–17 season, the Oilers named McDavid captain at 19 years, 266 days old, making him the youngest captain in NHL history. Edmonton also brought back Wayne Gretzky as partner and vice-chairman of Oilers Entertainment Group, with the unofficial title of mentor to McDavid.

As the Second Coming in Edmonton, whom fans call McJesus, McDavid led the league with 70 assists and won the Art Ross Trophy with an even 100 points in his sophomore season, 11 ahead of Crosby. At just 20 years old McDavid received the Hart Trophy as MVP.

For the first time in a decade, the Oilers were back in the playoffs. Fans filled the arena to watch road games and bought tickets to simply occupy the concourse when the Oilers were at home. Edmonton beat the San Jose Sharks in the first round, and in the second round Anaheim Ducks coach Randy Carlyle paid McDavid the biggest compliment an opponent can when he suggested the referees were giving the captain the "white glove treatment."

McDavid didn't bring the Stanley Cup back to the city in 2017, but he did give the world one of the all-time best awkward fan photos. It appears to be a hostage picture, with a couple holding his arms as he stares at the camera with a look of fear and confusion.

It's not a question of being aloof — the shy McDavid is the personification of aw-shucks — it's just that posing with fans is the only thing in hockey he hasn't mastered by the age of 20. He probably spent the off-season practicing in the mirror.

BRENT BURNS

The list of things that Brent Burns is at or near the top of in the NHL includes thickest beard, most teeth missing, most tattoo coverage, largest menagerie and points scored.

Looking through his annual NHL photo is like going through a flipbook of a Teen Wolf transformation. And yes, his body is a colorful mosaic of art and he once had 300 or so snakes, including some rare varieties he crossbred. But focusing on his eccentricities does a disservice to the work ethic that propelled Burns to the NHL. "He wasn't a very elegant skater. He was bent over like a hunchback toward the ice," recalled Jari Byrski, a skills coach who first met Burns when he was 8 years old. "The thing with Brent is he was always about energy. I'm not talking about a

crazy kid not paying attention. Absolutely not. When he set out to do something, he did it the right way and didn't go halfway. He was all in."

Burns was a 5-foot-11 winger when the Brampton Battalion chose him in the third round of the 2001 Ontario Hockey League draft. When training camp started, he was 6-foot-2. "I still think of myself as a small player," said Burns, who is now 6-foot-5 and 230 pounds. "I think it helped my skating and my puckhandling."

After Burns played just one season at forward with the Battalion in 2002–03, the Minnesota Wild took him with the 20th overall selection in the 2003 entry draft. He made quite a first impression, walking on stage in a white suit. "He looked like the guys from *Dumb and Dumber*," said Brampton coach Stan Butler.

Burns also impressed in his first NHL training camp. He made the Wild, and his legend began to grow in Minnesota. Off the ice he became known for his esoteric pursuits like Eastern culture and martial arts, as well as for growing his hair and collecting reptiles; on the ice he'd been converted into a defensemen and set a team record for blue-liners in 2010–11 with 46 points.

Then, in a draft day deal in 2011, the Wild sent Burns and a second-round draft pick to the San Jose Sharks for Devin Setoguchi, Charlie Coyle and a first-round pick.

The Sharks moved Burns back to forward during the 2012–13 season, but soon realized they were better served with him on the ice more frequently. In the three seasons between 2014 and 2017, the health and workout fanatic didn't miss a game and averaged almost 25 minutes of ice time.

In 2015–16 Burns set a new career high with 75 points and became just the fourth defenseman in the past 20 years to reach the 25-goal mark, scoring 27, many on his trademark snapshot that he favors over the booming slap shot. He also joined Bobby Orr and Ray Bourque as the only defensemen with at least 350 shots in a season — his 353 were second to Alex Ovechkin's 398.

In the first round of the 2016 playoffs the Sharks faced the Los Angeles Kings, their playoff tormentors, who had eliminated them in 2013 and 2014. Burns had eight points in the five-game series victory, and finished the postseason with 24 points in 24 games as the Sharks reached their first Stanley Cup Final, ultimately losing to the Pittsburgh Penguins.

Burns spent the off-season roaming the United States on his custom-made all-black road bicycle, while his family followed in their matte black Mercedes van. He'd work out in Wal-Mart parking lots and at the homes of people they met along the way. Finding his own Route 88 was a way to free his mind and spirit, while pushing his body outside the confines of a gym.

It paid off for Burns in 2016–17. The Barrie,

Ontario, native led all defensemen with 29 goals, 12 more than the next blue-liner, and 76 points, and he was first in the NHL with 320 shots.

"Right now, he's the best offensive defenseman in the league," according to Sharks coach Peter DeBoer. "And he's not giving up his defensive responsibilities to do it."

Norris Trophy voters agreed, naming him the 2017 winner. It was recognition that the self-described "goofy donkey" is more than a toothless yeti whose beard has inspired multiple Twitter accounts and a Chia Pet giveaway. He's quite simply one of the NHL's best players.

Played in four NHL All-Star Games (2011, 2015, 2016, 2017)	
Won gold at the 2015 World Championship and named best defenseman	
Won the 2016 World Cup of Hockey	
Won the Norris Trophy in 2017	

DREW DOUGHTY

Won gold at the 2008 World Junior Championship

Won gold at the 2010 and 2014 Olympics

Won the Stanley Cup twice (2012, 2014)

Won the Norris Trophy in 2016

Won the World Cup of Hockey in 2016

Exhibit A in the argument for east coast bias is the Kings' Drew Doughty. If hockey writers in the east couldn't stay up late enough to get a true measure of the talent in the west, they were missing out on one of the league's best players in Los Angeles.

Doughty's 2016 Norris Trophy as the NHL's best defenseman was years overdue, but the individual bauble was just icing on the cake. He'd already won every important championship (some twice) by the time it finally came his way.

Growing up in London, Ontario, Doughty dreamt of hoisting the World or FA Cups just as much as Lord Stanley's. His mother, Connie, is Portuguese and his father, Paul, is English, so soccer was a household passion.

Though Doughty was a standout soccer goalie, he made the difficult decision to focus on hockey at the age of 15. "I was just as good at soccer as I was at hockey," recalled Doughty. "But living in Canada, it's going to be tough to make it [in soccer] anywhere. So I kind of gave it up. I miss playing it all the time."

Paul believes the two sports worked together in Doughty's favor: "I actually think playing soccer helped him with hockey. He could sit back in net and watch the whole play develop in front of him."

At 17, Doughty led the Ontario Hockey League's Guelph Storm in scoring in 2006–07, with 74 points in 67 games. A year later he won the Max Kaminsky Trophy as the OHL's most outstanding defenseman and was named the top blue-liner at the 2008 World Junior Championship after Canada won gold.

Doughty was the second overall pick in the 2008 entry draft, and after his fitness was questioned he dropped 20 pounds during the summer. He made the team out of training camp and played his first game for the Kings at 18, the second-youngest defenseman in team history. Conditioning wasn't an issue; Doughty averaged almost 24 minutes a game his rookie year. "It's not junior anymore," said Sean O'Donnell, Doughty's first NHL defense partner and

mentor. "Playing against men, you'll get fatigued and that's when you get hurt.

"[Doughty] understood the game, he understood the nuances. It usually takes defensemen years to do that and some never get it. To see him do that as a 19-year-old, you knew he was special."

In 2010 Doughty was a finalist for the Norris at 20 years old, the second youngest to be nominated for the award after Bobby Orr. He had helped the Kings reach the playoffs for the first time in eight years. He was also the youngest member of Canada's gold medal Olympic team. Over the course of the tournament he moved up the depth chart to form the team's top defense tandem with Duncan Keith.

Two years later, as the Kings steamrolled their way to the franchise's first championship, Doughty's 16 points in 20 playoff games led all blue-liners, and his 26:08 of average ice time was almost a minute more than anyone else in the Stanley Cup Final.

In 2014, after adding a second gold medal to his trophy case at the Sochi Olympics, Doughty topped all defenseman again with 18 points, and the Kings won their second Stanley Cup.

The 2016–17 season started with more international titles, this time at the World Cup of Hockey, but ended with the Kings on the outside of the playoffs looking in. Although he didn't have another Norris-caliber season, Doughty was more concerned with getting the Kings back to into Stanley Cup form. "It was a great honor to win that award. I had a lot of great teammates around me and great coaching staff, great organization to help me win that," Doughty said. "It's disappointing that I didn't have the year I would have liked to have had and be up for it again, but that's not what I'm about. I'm about trying to make this team make the playoffs and win championships, and that's all I worry about."

JONATHAN QUICK

Let's put the 2016–17 season aside; it was a write-off for Jonathan Quick and his Los Angeles Kings. It was essentially lost for the goaltender in the first period of the first game, and it's no coincidence that the perennial Stanley Cup contenders failed to qualify for the playoffs.

After severely injuring his groin against the San Jose Sharks, the same problem that kept him out for almost two months in 2013, Quick returned to play 17 games toward the end of the season, adding a handful of wins to the Kings record that he owns.

Born in 1986, Quick wasn't living up to his name in his first two years of organized hockey, so he thought he'd try playing goal at the tender age of 7. He honed his skills the old fashioned way, on his street in Milford, Connecticut, with his friends and neighbors. He went on to play at Hamden High School and Avon Old Farms, where he had a 45-3 record, led the team to consecutive New England Prep School Championships and recorded nine shut-outs in his senior year, a New England prep school record. "I remember he was an athletic, impressive freshman goalie, but geez, he was just a tiny kid," said Bill Verneris, the Hamden coach. "Then as a sophomore he started to grow and beat out the senior who had been the starter on the varsity team.

"In his first game, against one of the best teams in the state, we're winning and Jon is playing great. With 20 seconds left in the game, a player on the other team gets a breakaway. He makes a couple fakes and gets Jon sprawled on his back. But when he shoots, Jon reaches up and snatches the puck out of the air with his glove — pulls it back out of the net. That's where it all began. People in Hamden still talk about that incredible save."

Drafted in 2005 by the Kings in the third round, 72nd overall, Quick went to University of Massachusetts-Amherst, where he had a .920 save percentage in his sophomore season and helped the Minutemen reach their first ever NCAA tournament.

Quick went pro after his second year, splitting the 2007–08 season between the American Hockey League's Manchester Monarchs and the Reading Royals of the East Coast Hockey League, where he was demoted for oversleeping and missing a team meeting. He made the best of it, becoming the second goalie to get a shutout and score a goal in his first ECHL game, after fellow NHL goalie Mike Smith.

Quick got into three games for the Kings that season and played 44 in 2008–09. He set a career high and a franchise record the following season with 72 games played. His 39 wins also set a new team record, which he broke in 2015–16 with 40. Proving he'd reached elite level, Quick was also named to Team USA for the 2010 Vancouver Olympics, earning a silver medal as one of Ryan Miller's backups.

In 2011–12 Quick played in his first All-Star Game and was a Vezina Trophy finalist. In the playoffs he led all goalies with a 1.41 goals-against average and a gaudy .946 save percentage as the Kings won their first Stanley Cup, capturing the Conn Smythe Trophy as playoff MVP. Two years later he backstopped the Kings to their second title after he won the William Jennings Trophy for allowing the fewest goals during the regular season.

Quick also became the Kings' career leader in victories in 2014, and he was sitting at 260 wins at the end of the 2016–17 season, including one in his first game back after 59 games on the sideline. An anxious Staples Center crowd gave Quick a standing ovation when he was introduced. "It was exciting for everybody — players, coaches, fans," said former coach Darryl Sutter of Quick's return. "It was fun to see. He's an emotional leader in a lot of ways for our hockey club. It's good to have him back in the room."

Sutter set a Kings record for coaching wins with the victory, but it was too little, too late for the team and the brass. Sutter and general manager Dean Lombardi were let go when the season ended without a playoff appearance.

The 2016–17 season was one to forget, but the Los Angeles faithful can still count on a solid foundation of players and their unorthodox, athletic goaltender as the bedrock.

Won silver at the 2010 Olympics

Won the Stanley Cup twice (2012, 2014)

Won the Conn Smythe Trophy in 2012

Played in two NHL All-Star Games (2012, 2016)

Won the William Jennings Trophy in 2014

JOE PAVELSKI

Won silver at the 2010 Olympics

Played in two NHL All-Star Games (2016, 2017)

Led the NHL with 11 game-winning goals in 2015–16

Captained Team USA at the 2016 World Cup of Hockey

Joe Pavelski was an afterthought in the 2003 entry draft. He wasn't even the San Jose Sharks' first pick in the seventh round; at 201st overall that honor went to Jonathan Tremblay, a winger with one point and 232 penalty minutes in the Quebec Major Junior Hockey League.

Pavelski was taken four spots after him. Playing in Iowa for the Waterloo Black Hawks of the United States Hockey League, he was undersized at 5-foot-11 and not the most fleet of foot. "He can't skate, he's not big enough. He can't skate, he's not big enough," recalled Black Hawks coach P.K. O'Handley of the repetitive knock on Pavelski. But "his hockey IQ, even at 17, was off the chart."

He was also a winner. From Plover, Wisconsin, Pavelski led Stevens Point Area High School to a state championship in 2002 and helped the Black Hawks win the USHL's Clark Cup in 2004.

Pavelski joined the University of Wisconsin for the 2004–05 season and in his sophomore year he led the team in assists (33) and points (56) as the Badgers won the 2006 Frozen Four championship. "It's his hands and the six inches between his ears that really elevate his play," according to Wisconsin coach Mike Eaves. "The other thing that has been a part of his success is his attention to detail in his game. He's just got that desire to keep getting better and that's why he continues to improve."

Pavelski turned pro in 2006 and had 26 points in just 16 games with the Worcester Sharks in the American Hockey League. He was called up to San Jose, never to return, and scored a goal in his NHL debut. "You could tell he was special from the get-go," said Worcester coach Roy Sommer. "I've been doing this a long time and there are certain players that you get and you go, 'Man this guy is going to do great things,' and that's what he did."

In 2008–09, Pavelski had 25 goals and 59 points. It was the first of eight straight years and counting with at least 20 goals (not including the lockout season of 2012–13). In 2010 he proved that

he belonged among the best in the world at the Vancouver Olympics. Down a goal to the Canadians in the gold medal game, Pavelski won the faceoff for the U.S. and held the offensive zone for Zach Parise's late equalizer. The Americans lost in overtime but Pavelski went home with a silver medal and a new level of self-confidence.

Four years later Pavelski played for Team USA again at the Sochi Olympics, during a season in which he became the fourth player in Sharks history to reach 40 goals (41). He was named to the 2013–14 Second All-Star Team and won the Sharks' Player of the Year award.

But in the 2014 playoffs, San Jose blew a 3-0 first-round series lead and lost to the Los Angeles Kings. As a result, the Sharks stripped Joe Thornton of the captaincy, and after a year of rotating alternates named Pavelski captain in 2015.

In his first year as official leader, Pavelski finished fifth in the NHL with 38 goals and appeared in his first All-Star Game. And after years of San Jose underachieving in the playoffs, he had nine points in six games in the Western Conference Final to take the Sharks to the 2016 Stanley Cup Final, the first in franchise history, where they lost in six games to the Pittsburgh Penguins. "All he cares about is winning," said coach Peter DeBoer. "There's not a selfish bone in his body as far as his own personal numbers or agenda. It's all about winning. Where do you find guys that get 100 points and block shots and kill penalties and win faceoffs and go to the dirty areas of the ice? You can count on one hand the number of guys in the league that do that."

After finishing one goal shy of his fifth 30-goal season in 2016–17, the 205th draft pick trails just Alex Ovechkin and Steven Stamkos, both first overall selections, in goals over the past five seasons.

Not that Pavelski is keeping track.

COREY PERRY

There's little left for Corey Perry to accomplish in hockey, but that doesn't mean his fire has dimmed. At 32 he still knows how to score and, more importantly, how to win, even if that means running afoul of NHL law.

Ironically his father was a police officer. Corey was born in New Liskeard, Ontario, and the family moved to Peterborough when he was 10. At 15 he led the Peterborough Petes bantam AAA team to the OHL Cup, a tournament for teams from Canada and the U.S., with 20 points in eight games.

It was a sign of things to come for Perry, who was just 5-foot-11 and 148 pounds when the London Knights selected him fifth overall in the 2001 Ontario Hockey League draft. "They had to take me

separately to do the bench press because I couldn't get 135 pounds off my chest," Perry recalled of the pre-draft workout. But by his final year of major junior Perry had put some meat on his bones and added more trophies to his shelf.

The Knights set a record by starting the 2004–05 season with a 29-0-2 unbeaten streak, and finished it with the OHL title and the Memorial Cup. Perry led the OHL in scoring on his way to being named Most Outstanding Player, and he won the MVP award in both the OHL playoffs and Memorial Cup.

Perry was also a member of one of the greatest teams ever assembled for the World Junior tournament. He made the 2005 team as the 13th forward but worked his way onto the top line with Sidney

Crosby and Patrice Bergeron. The trio combined for almost half of Canada's goals en route to the gold.

The Anaheim Ducks had drafted Perry 28th overall in 2003, but he didn't make his NHL debut until 2005–06. Up to 6-foot-3 and over 200 pounds, Perry played his first full season in 2006–07. In the playoffs he tied for second on the team with 15 points, and his goal in Game 5 of the Stanley Cup Final clinched the franchise's first championship.

In 2010 Perry was named to Team Canada for the Olympics and scored four goals in seven games, including Canada's second in the gold medal game that was won on Crosby's Golden Goal. "Going into overtime in that game and knowing what was at stake … [winning] with family and friends watching … made it that much sweeter," said Perry.

After leading the Ducks in goals for three consecutive seasons, Perry won the 2011 Maurice Richard Trophy with 50 goals. He also finished third in scoring with 98 points and was recognized as the NHL's best player with the Hart Trophy. "He's been a little bit underrated," said Ducks coach Randy Carlyle during the 2010–11 season. "[Critics] say Corey can't skate, he can't do this…. It's always been more about what he can't do than what he can do. Now he's proving to them all that he can do everything."

Perry won another gold medal at the 2014 Olympics, and in 2016 he joined the Triple Gold Club when he captained Canada to the World Championship. With his World Junior title, Memorial Cup and Stanley Cup he became the second player to win all five, after former Ducks teammate Scott Niedermayer. A few months later he added yet another title to his collection at the 2016 World Cup of Hockey.

Universally admired for his unprecedented success, Perry has also made enemies along the way. He's not afraid to create space for himself — he's the Ducks' career leader in penalty minutes — and teammates have called him Worm and Slime for his ability to get to the dirty areas in front of the goalie.

He slithered through the crease in Game 4 of the second round of the 2017 playoffs against the Edmonton Oilers, a hotly debated play when Perry grazed the face of goalie Cam Talbot. It allowed Ryan Getzlaf to score on the way to an overtime victory. Two days later he assisted on a pair of goals in the final three minutes of the game, including one with 15 seconds left, as the Ducks overcame a 3–0 deficit. He then scored the double-overtime winner.

After receiving the official Key to the City of Peterborough in 2014 not much is missing from Perry's trophy shelf, apart from the Lady Byng for sportsmanship and gentlemanly play. But no one is holding their breath on that one.

Won gold at the 2005 World Junior Championship

Won the Stanley Cup in 2007

Won the Hart Trophy and Maurice Richard Trophy in 2011

Won gold at the 2010 and 2014 Olympics

Won the World Cup of Hockey and gold at the World Championship in 2016

JOHNNY GAUDREAU

Won gold at the 2013 World Junior Championship

Won the 2014 Hobey Baker Award

Named to the NHL All-Rookie Team in 2015

Played in three NHL All-Star Games (2015, 2016, 2017)

Won the Lady Byng Trophy in 2017

Johnny Hockey's nickname began as a play on Johnny Football's. It invokes the youthful exuberance that both Johnnys displayed while tearing up the collegiate ranks in their respective sports. While Texas A&M quarterback Johnny Manziel's immaturity landed him more on *TMZ* than *Monday Night Football*, Johnny Gaudreau has proven he's legit, even though he still looks like a kid.

The native of Salem, New Jersey, was a child prodigy, skating rings around older kids. When Jane Gaudreau suggested to her husband, Guy, that Johnny might be in the NHL some day, Guy tempered expectations: "Whoa, you sound like some of my crazy hockey parents. He's not going to the NHL."

Guy knew what he was talking about. A member of the athletic hall of fame at Norwich University in Vermont, he was hockey director at Hollydell Ice Arena, where Johnny learned to skate.

Still dominating while at Gloucester Catholic High School, Gaudreau joined the Dubuque Fighting Saints of the United States Hockey League in 2010–11. The 17-year-old scored 72 points in 60 games and earned Rookie of the Year.

That convinced the Calgary Flames, who drafted Gaudreau in the fourth round in 2011, 104th overall, well ahead of Central Scouting's projection of 193rd overall. At 5-foot-6 and 137 pounds, even that projection was generous for a winger of his size.

Gaudreau chose to hone his game (and grow) at Boston College, winning the NCAA title in his freshman year after being cut from USA Hockey's 2012 World Junior team. "He takes those setbacks, uses them to motivate him more and it has furthered his determination," said Boston College associate head coach Greg Brown about the USA Hockey snub. "He is an incredibly competitive kid. Every day in practice, every little small game we play, you can see the fire come out in him." Gaudreau made the team in 2013 and led the tournament with seven goals en route to the U.S. winning gold.

A Hobey Baker finalist as a sophomore, Gaudreau

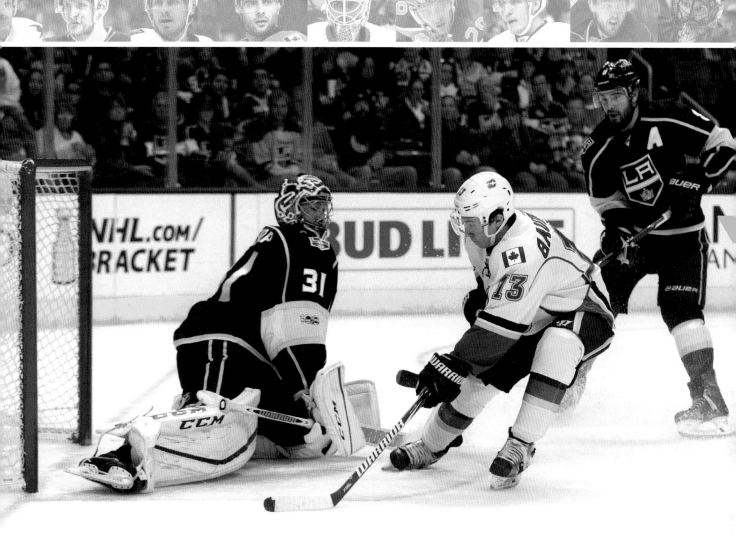

stuck around Boston College to play another year with younger brother Matt in 2013–14. He won the national player of the year award as a junior and the next day signed with the Flames. The team welcomed him in style, flying him out by private jet to their last game of the 2013–14 season. Gaudreau repaid them with a goal on his first NHL shot.

Gaudreau ended his first full season with 24 goals. He led all rookies in assists with 40, tied for the rookie lead in points with 64, recorded 14 multiple-point games and was a finalist for the Calder Trophy. He also played in the All-Star Game and helped Calgary reach the playoffs for the first time in six years, leading the team with nine points in 11 games. Gaudreau followed that up with 30 goals and 78 points in 2015–16, which was good for sixth in league scoring.

After four points in three games with Team North America at the 2016 World Cup of Hockey, Gaudreau skipped training camp over a contract impasse. He eventually signed a six-year, $40.5 mil-

lion contract but had a slow start to the season. He rebounded for 61 points, his third All-Star Game appearance, a second trip to the playoffs and the Lady Byng Trophy, awarded for sportsmanship and gentlemanly conduct.

It's a remarkable feat, considering those who can't catch him, slash him. "It's tough to play through, obviously," said Gaudreau. "No one likes getting slashed on the wrist or in the back of the legs.

"Thankfully, I've been learning from it my whole career. You've just got to try to create offense and find a way to put the puck in the back of the net. That'll ultimately shut them up and make them stop doing that."

Flames captain Mark Giordano said it doesn't bother the diminutive winger: "He gives it back quite often. He's going to go back at guys and not back down. But the bottom line is, when he gets the puck on his stick, that's when he's most intimidating."

OLIVER EKMAN-LARSSON

PACIFIC DIVISION
Coyotes | Defense | 23

As a kid growing up in tiny Tingsryd, Sweden, Oliver Oscar Emanuel Ekman-Larsson would set his VCR to tape Detroit Red Wings games that were on late at night so he could watch them the next day after school.

It was a stacked Wings roster with several future Hall of Famers and Swedes, including their statesman and engine from the back, Nicklas Lidstrom. He was Ekman-Larsson's favorite player and the model for his game growing up.

Defense runs in the family — Ekman-Larsson's grandfather played on the blue line for Sweden at the 1972 Olympics in Sapporo, Japan — but he took a shot at center when his dad coached him because his father wanted him to see the ice from a different perspective. He moved back to defense when he joined a higher age group, with a better understanding of the passes his forwards wanted.

At 17 Ekman-Larsson joined Leksands in Sweden's second division, scoring 17 points in 39 games in the 2008–09 season, a league record for players 18 and under. The following year his 27 points led all teenagers in the second division.

The Phoenix Coyotes liked what they saw in Lidstrom-lite and drafted him sixth overall in 2009. In 2010 he won bronze medals with Sweden at both the World Juniors and World Championship and then played his first NHL game.

Ekman-Larsson never got the chance to man the blue line with his idol, but in 2011 he did share a dressing room when he was picked by Team Lidstrom to compete in the skills competition at the NHL All-Star Game.

By the time the 2014 Olympics in Sochi, Russia, came around, Lidstrom had retired and Ekman-Larsson was a rising star in both the NHL and his country. He had three points and was a plus-4 in the tournament — good for second best on the team — as Sweden captured the silver medal.

Back in the desert, Ekman-Larsson finished with 23 goals in 2013–14 to tie Phil Housley's franchise mark for goals by a defenseman and set the record for most goals in a season by a Swedish-born defenseman. In the 2014–15 season he led all NHL defensemen in goals, game-winning goals and power-play goals.

Ekman-Larsson's 43 points in 2014–15 led the Coyotes, and he was the team's top scorer again in 2015–16 with 55 points. He also set an NHL record for defensemen with eight game-winning goals. Being an NHL team's leading scorer twice in a row is a rare feat for any defenseman not named Bobby Orr.

Now midway through a six-year extension signed in 2013 that pays him $5.5 million a year and only just entering his prime, Ekman-Larsson was called "the best deal in hockey right now," by a Western Conference executive in 2016, while also remaining one of the league's best-kept secrets.

In 2016–17 Ekman-Larsson's upward trajectory dipped a little, the result of playing with a broken left thumb for six weeks while trudging toward a fifth straight season out of the playoffs. He didn't miss a single game while his thumb healed, and he didn't make excuses. "I felt like I could still be out on the ice and adapt my game to that situation," said Ekman-Larsson. "I think that's something you will have as long as you play in the league, that you are able to battle through, and I've battled through a lot of stuff over the years. I feel that helps you, too, and realize you just have to find a way to be the best player every day, and you're not going to feel 100 percent every night."

Ekman-Larsson also had the benefit of watching how former Coyotes captain Shane Doan dealt with adversity in the NHL. "When I got in the league,

I looked to Doaner every game we lost and how he acted or how he handled himself. I think that's huge, especially when we have a lot of young players. I feel that's important."

With Doan now gone, the reins have been handed to Ekman-Larsson, and while the Coyotes are not the turn-of-the-21st century Red Wings, they do have a wealth of young talent and their own tall, smooth, puck-moving Swedish defenseman to steer the ship. And somewhere in Sweden another young defenseman is coming home after school to watch Ekman-Larsson's every move on YouTube.

Won silver at the 2014 Olympics
Led the Coyotes in scoring in 2014–15 and 2015–16
Holds the record for most goals in an NHL season by a Swedish-born defenseman with 23
Set the NHL record for game-winning goals by a defenseman with eight in 2015–16

MARK GIORDANO

- Named to the CHL All-Rookie Team in 2003
- Named captain of the Calgary Flames in 2013
- Played in two NHL All-Star Games (2015, 2016)
- Received the NHL Foundation Player Award in 2016

As the Battle of Alberta reawakens — both the Calgary Flames and the Edmonton Oilers made the 2017 playoffs — the two provincial captains are diametrically opposed.

While the Oilers are captained by flashy 20-year-old Connor McDavid, the Flames' Mark Giordano is a no-nonsense defenseman, a late bloomer who's approaching his mid-30s. Their paths to the NHL couldn't have been more different. McDavid is a wunderkind who was pegged for success as an adolescent and an instant superstar. Giordano, not so much.

A Toronto, Ontario, native, Giordano went undrafted in 2001, which wasn't surprising since he hadn't played any major junior hockey. He approached local York University about catching on with the varsity team but ended up walking on to the Owen Sound Attack of the Ontario Hockey League as a 19-year-old after a tryout.

Two Calgary scouts saw potential in Giordano and recommended him to then-general manager Darryl Sutter after receiving glowing reports from Owen Sound's coach and GM. "My first contract was a three-way contract — NHL, AHL and ECHL," explained Giordano. "Darryl Sutter was honest. He said, 'This is pretty much a take-it-or-leave-it-offer.' But he also said, 'If you play well enough, I don't care where you were drafted, or if you were drafted, you'll get a chance.'"

Giordano took the offer and debuted in 2005–06. Early the next season he played his first NHL game in Toronto and the first his parents were able to watch in person. It was a memorable night for Maple Leafs fans. Mats Sundin scored his 500th career goal, to complete his hat trick, and was chosen first star.

Lost among the celebrations were Giordano's first and second career NHL goals. "It was a great game," recalled Giordano. "I was second star. Sundin got first star and I got second, and I remember coming out and I got booed. But I came out because I knew there were so many people from my family there."

Giordano split the next two seasons between the

Flames and their American Hockey League affiliate. In 2007–08, after his Flames contract expired, he accepted a one-year deal with Moscow Dynamo of the Kontinental Hockey League. "It's sort of how I've always done things in my career," said Giordano. "The risky things, I always believed they would work out, if you worked hard and played well enough."

It was worth the gamble; after that season Calgary offered him a three-year deal with no minor league provisions, and Giordano has been a regular on the blue line since. In 2013 the undrafted defenseman succeeded future Hall of Famer Jarome Iginla as captain.

Private and low-key off the ice, Giordano commands respect in the dressing room. "He leads by example," said Flames head coach Glen Gulutzan. "He is not afraid to put the team in front of himself. He's a great human being. I just think we're very fortunate here — and I'm very fortunate — to have such a good leader."

In 2014–15, the defense-first Giordano also added some offense. He was leading all defensemen in scoring and was a Norris Trophy favorite when a bicep tear in a February game ended his season.

Giordano bounced back the following year with 21 goals and 35 assists in 82 games, finishing third in team scoring and tying for second among NHL defensemen in goals (with 21) and sixth in points (with 56). And in 2016–17 he missed just one game and was a plus-22 for the playoff-bound Flames. "When I first broke into the league, I didn't understand why Darryl and all the other GMs stress experience," said Giordano. "Now I do. It truly makes you a better player, especially as a defenseman. You're calmer in your own zone. You don't run around as much as you get older, and you read plays better. I think the guys who come into the league and are elite defensemen at a young age are special, special players."

Sometimes it just takes a little extra time to prove how special you are.

MARTIN JONES

Just a few years after donning the pads full time Martin Jones played at the prestigious Quebec International Pee-Wee Tournament, where players like Guy Lafleur, Wayne Gretzky and Steven Stamkos made a name for themselves.

Every year thousands of fans and scores of scouts come to watch 11- and 12-year-olds, hoping to catch a glimpse of future NHL stars. In 2003 they saw a cool young Jones lead his North Shore Winter Club Winterhawks to one of the divisional titles.

"When you watched him play, you literally wouldn't know if he had a shutout or had let in four," said Billy Coupland, Jones' coach for five years. "It was like he was back home playing in front of friends and family."

In 2005 the North Vancouver team won the bantam provincial title and Jones allowed just a single goal in six games in the year-end tournament. Over five seasons together the Winterhawks went 98-2 in the Pacific Coast Amateur Hockey Association and won the league title each year.

Still just 5-foot-8 when he was eligible for the Western Hockey League draft in 2005, Jones wasn't taken until the fourth round by the Calgary Hitmen. He was relegated to the backup role, where he remained in 2008 when he was passed over in the NHL entry draft. "He was disappointed," said his father, Harvey. "But he doesn't let things like that knock him. He wouldn't accept failure."

By then Jones had grown to 6-foot-4 and earned

a tryout with the Los Angeles Kings, in part because his former backup in North Vancouver was Dylan Crawford, son of LA coach Marc Crawford. Jones impressed and was offered an entry-level contract.

Sent back to the WHL Jones inherited the number one job with the Hitmen and ran with it. In 2010 he won the WHL's best goaltender and playoff MVP awards on his way to being named the top goaltender at the Memorial Cup.

After four years in junior the Kings had Jones apprentice in the American Hockey League with the Manchester Monarchs for three and a half seasons. He finally made his NHL debut on December 3, 2013, a victory over the Anaheim Ducks, and then reeled off seven more wins in a row, which tied the record for most consecutive wins to start a career set by the Philadelphia Flyers' Bob Froese in 1982–83. Over that stretch Jones had a 0.98 goals-against average, a .966 save percentage and three shutouts.

Jones played 19 games backing up Jonathan Quick in 2013–14, with a 1.81 goals-against average, .934 save percentage and four shutouts. He also played 56 minutes over two games in the playoffs to get his named etched on the Stanley Cup with the 2014 champion Kings.

With Quick ensconced as the Kings starter, Jones was traded in June 2015 — twice. First he was sent to the Boston Bruins as part of the deal that brought Milan Lucic to Los Angeles; four days later the Bruins traded him to the San Jose Sharks for a prospect and a first-round draft pick. The Sharks immediately signed him to a three-year, $9 million contract to make him their starter. "Martin was at the top of our list of players that we had targeted," said Sharks general manager Doug Wilson. "We're extremely excited to have him on board."

Wilson's excitement was justified as Jones set a franchise record with a shutout streak of 234 minutes and 33 seconds in October 2015. He finished the season third in the NHL with 37 wins and second with six shutouts.

But it was in the playoffs that he really thrilled. Jones had back-to-back shutouts in the Western Conference Final against the St. Louis Blues to help the Sharks reach their first Stanley Cup Final. He made 44 saves in Game 5, the most in an elimination game in Stanley Cup Final history, before the Sharks bowed out in six games to the Pittsburgh Penguins. "He looks so calm in there," said teammate Joe Thornton after the Sharks beat the Blues. "I love that."

A year later the Sharks were eliminated in the first round by the Edmonton Oilers, despite Jones' .935 save percentage and 1.75 goals-against average.

Since peewee Jones has played like he has ice in his veins, and it hasn't melted in the California heat.

Named the WHL's best goaltender and playoff MVP in 2010

Named best goaltender at the Memorial Cup in 2010

Won the Stanley Cup in 2014

Played in the 2017 NHL All-Star Game

29 ♠

LEON DRAISAITL

PACIFIC DIVISION | Oilers | Center

29 ♥

He was called the German Gretzky before he'd ever suited up for Edmonton, but when Leon Draisaitl did pull on the Oilers' jersey he made like Mark Messier.

Edmonton drafted Draisaitl third overall from the Western Hockey League's Prince Albert Raiders in 2014. In his first 37 NHL games in 2014–15, Draisaitl had just two goals and seven assists, so the Oilers sent him down to the Kelowna Rockets, who had traded for his rights. Back in junior he was named playoff MVP after his 28 points in 19 post-season games sent Kelowna to the Memorial Cup.

The Rockets lost in overtime in the championship game to the Oshawa Generals, but Draisaitl led the Memorial Cup in scoring with four goals and seven

points in five games and won the Stafford Smythe Memorial Trophy as tournament MVP.

The following season Draisaitl played just six games with the Bakersfield Condors in the American Hockey League before Edmonton called him up. He scored seven goals and 10 assists in his first 10 games, which made him the first Oiler to start a season with 17 points in 10 games since Messier in 1989–90.

Draisaitl worked on his strength and conditioning in the off-season, and playing with renewed confidence in 2015–16 he finished with 19 goals and 51 points in 72 games. The Oilers missed the playoffs for the 10th straight season, but they had the new Messier to their young Gretzky.

Oilers captain Connor McDavid is the man in Edmonton, Draisaitl the wingman. In a literal sense, Draisaitl plays on McDavid's right side when he's not centering the second line.

The 2016–17 season was a rebirth for the franchise. Playing in a new arena, the Oilers tied for seventh overall in the NHL and Draisaitl finished eighth in the league with 77 points, on 29 goals and 48 assists.

One person who was not a fan of Draisaitl's breakthrough was the Buffalo Sabres' Jack Eichel. With a goal and an assist in the regular season finale, Draisaitl averaged 0.939 points per game, which was 10th in the NHL. If Eichel had finished in the top 10 he would have collected a $2 million bonus, but he finished 11th with 0.934 points per game, missing out by 5/1,000ths of a decimal point.

Draisaitl would have his own heart broken a few weeks later. After dispatching the defending Western Conference champion San Jose Sharks in six games in the first round, the Oilers pushed the Anaheim Ducks to Game 7 in the Western Conference semifinals.

In Game 5 the Oilers were up 3–0, but allowed three goals in the final 3:16 of the third period before

losing in double overtime. Following that devastating loss, Edmonton came out on fire in Game 6, led by Draisaitl. He had the first playoff hat trick by an Oiler since 2000 and two assists in the 7–1 win, putting him second in playoff scoring with 16 points, one behind the Pittsburgh Penguins' Evgeni Malkin. In 11 games against Anaheim in the regular season and playoffs he had 11 goals and 21 points. "He's been a horse," said teammate Zack Kassian. "Everyone knows how good he is in here. Sometimes he doesn't get enough credit because he plays with [Connor McDavid]. But we all know what he's capable of."

Selected third overall in the 2014 NHL entry draft

Named WHL playoff MVP in 2015

Named MVP at the 2015 Memorial Cup

Runner-up at the 2016 World Cup of Hockey

Despite a devastating loss in Game 7 and a long season that started with being runner-up at the 2016 World Cup of Hockey, Draisaitl accepted Germany's invitation to join them at the 2017 World Championship. Three days after being bounced from the postseason he was playing in Lanxess Arena in Cologne, the city where he was born when his father, Peter, was playing for the Cologne Sharks. Draisaitl was named one of Germany's top three players, despite dressing in only three of their eight games. "Playing for Germany is very important to him," said German teammate and New York Islander Dennis Seidenberg. "Every kid watches those games and looks up to him and one day they want to be like him."

Now, after a spring of renewed hope, kids in northern Alberta are dreaming of one day being called the Canadian Draisaitl.

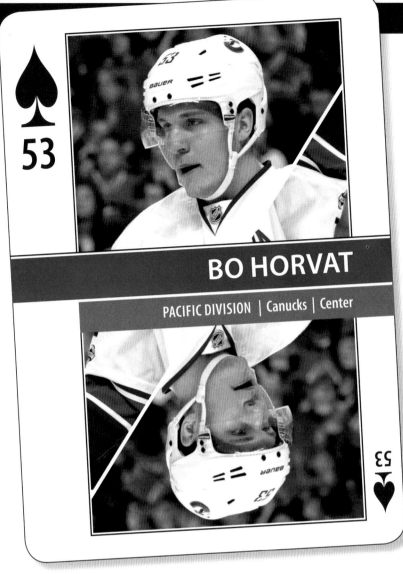

BO HORVAT

PACIFIC DIVISION | Canucks | Center

It was draft déjà vu for Horvat in the NHL. Then-Vancouver Canucks general manager Mike Gillis shocked the hockey world by trading goaltender Cory Schneider, who had recently beaten out Roberto Luongo for the starting job, for the ninth spot in the 2013 draft and the right to take Horvat.

A few years later Gillis was replaced by former Canuck Trevor Linden as team president (in part because of his controversial trades), but it seems like he knew what he was doing all along.

Horvat suffered an injury in his first NHL training camp but showed enough for the Canucks to keep him around. At 19 he became the first teenager to play for the team since Ryan Kesler and he stayed with the big club instead of being allowed to play for Canada's World Junior team.

Once again he started from the bottom, on the fourth line, but earned his keep with strong faceoffs, shot blocking and a solid work ethic. Projected to be a future captain and shutdown center — high on hustle and low on highlights — he exceeded expectations and busted the predicted timeline.

Horvat has become a scorer; he led the Canucks with 55 points in the 2016 calendar year despite being seventh among forwards in even strength ice time. In 2016–17 he became the first player not named Sedin, Naslund or Bure to lead the Canucks in scoring in two decades.

Called a weak skater in junior, Horvat participated in the fastest skater competition at the 2017 All-Star Game. Teammate Luca Sbisa has seen the six-foot, 223-pound Horvat's foot speed increase since he was a rookie. "I think guys are still underestimating how fast he is," said Sbisa. "He burns a lot of guys wide. He's a powerful guy with a big body and silky hands. He's got a lot of tricks up his sleeve, and it's been really fun to watch him develop."

B o Horvat grew up in tiny Rodney, Ontario. Like many a precocious hockey player he had to leave his small town to find commensurate competition. For Horvat, that meant joining the Toronto Red Wings, a peewee AAA hockey club, at 12.

Major junior hockey brought him to the Ontario Hockey League powerhouse London Knights, the team his father, Tim, played for and a factory for turning out NHL players. As the ninth pick in the 2011 OHL draft Horvat started life in London, Ontario, as a fourth-liner, but by his second season he'd blossomed into a star. He earned the Wayne Gretzky 99 Award as OHL playoff MVP after scoring the overtime winner in Game 7 of the OHL final against the Barrie Colts to send his team to the 2013 Memorial Cup.

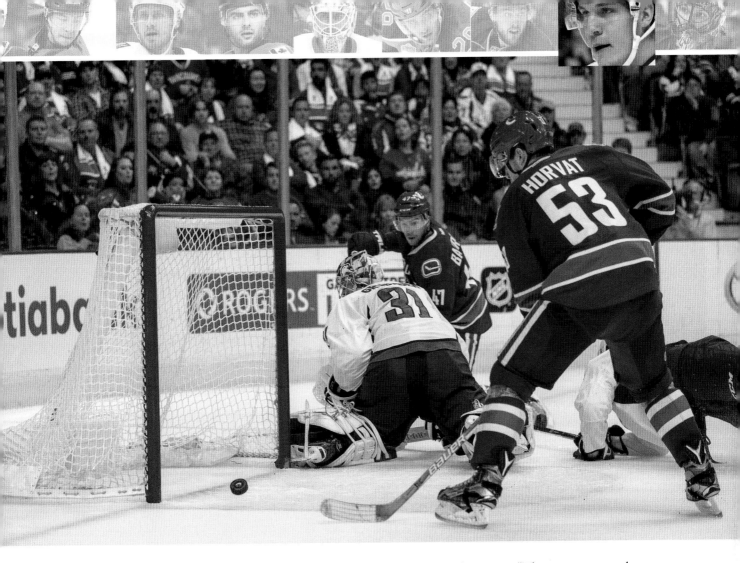

Horvat was the Canucks' only representative at the All-Star Game and the youngest to appear in one since Linden played at the age of 20.

"All those tweets about that being a bad trade is probably the worst thing [fans have said to me]," said Horvat. "The whole Schneider ordeal has kind of passed. He's doing great in New Jersey, and I've found my way in Van, so it's blown over."

After linemate Alexandre Burrows was traded to the Ottawa Senators at the 2017 trade deadline, Horvat ascended the leadership ladder and inherited an alternate captain role. In Daniel and Henrik Sedin he has the Canucks' all-time leaders in goals and points, respectively, to lean on.

The brothers took him aside during his 27-game goal drought in 2015–16 and told him how they'd gotten through their early career struggles. Their professionalism has rubbed off on him, not a given in a 21-year-old emerging star. "They've had the biggest impact on my career from a player

standpoint," said Horvat. "They come to work every day with smiles on their faces. They do unbelievable things in the community. It makes you want to be like them and help out that way."

And as predicted by the Swedish twins, the goalless streak was good for the kid, who will eventually take over for them. According to Horvat, "It made me the player I am right now … I've been there, done that with the mental side of it where I had to fight through that adversity. Having that early in my career really helped me and pushed me to be better."

Named OHL playoff MVP in 2013
Named the OHL's Most Sportsmanlike Player in 2013
Played in the 2017 NHL All-Star Game
Led the Canucks in scoring in 2016–17

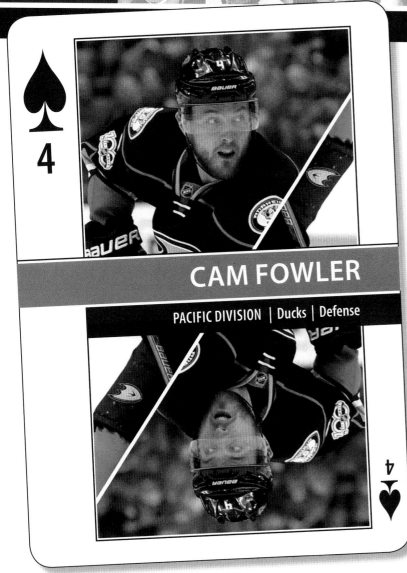

CAM FOWLER

PACIFIC DIVISION | Ducks | Defense

Cam Fowler grew up on both sides of the Detroit River. Perry Fowler is Canadian and his wife, Bridget, is American; Cameron was born in Windsor, Ontario, but moved to Farmington, Michigan, before he turned 2, where his two sisters were born. It's a cross-border family, and the game of hockey kept them busy on the Ambassador Bridge.

The young defenseman joined the Tier 1 Detroit HoneyBaked team at 14 and was drafted 18th overall by the Ontario Hockey League's Kitchener Rangers in 2007. But Fowler committed to the U.S. National Development Team program in Michigan instead, so the Rangers relinquished his rights and a year later the Windsor Spitfires picked him one spot earlier in the 2008 OHL draft.

Fowler remained with the NDTP for the 2008–09 season and starred at the 2009 World Under-18 Championship for the U.S. The Americans took home gold and Fowler was named best defenseman in the tournament.

He then joined the Spitfires for 2009–10 and put up 55 points in 55 OHL games. Mid-season, Fowler took a little hiatus over the holidays to join Team USA and beat Canada for gold at the 2010 World Juniors. "It was a huge experience for me," said Fowler. "Playing on the stage like that against the best players in the world and being able to perform and win the gold medal.

"It was Hockey Canada there for a long time with the streak they had, and for us to go into Canadian territory and take that gold medal was a really special feeling."

Fowler finished the dream season with an OHL title and the Memorial Cup, where he led all defensemen with six points in four tournament games.

Projected to go as high as third in the 2010 entry draft, and compared by Central Scouting to Brian Leetch and Phil Housley, both Hall of Famers, Fowler fell to the Anaheim Ducks at 12th overall. The knock on him was that he wasn't physical enough for the rigors of NHL life.

Ducks coach Randy Carlyle disagreed and put Fowler in the lineup immediately. He made his NHL debut on October 8, 2010, in his hometown against the Detroit Red Wings, becoming the Ducks' second-youngest player in franchise history at 18 years and 307 days old.

Fowler proved he belonged in the NHL, despite his callow youth. He scored a power-play goal in three straight games in November, making him the second rookie defenseman and the youngest defenseman in NHL history to do so. He was the only blue-liner in his draft year to spend the whole season

in the NHL, and he set Ducks records for goals (10) and points (40) by a rookie defenseman, as well as the team's rookie record for assists (30).

His first NHL season remained his best statistically, until Fowler was reunited with Carlyle in his second stint as Ducks coach. "We've tried to actually put more pressure on him this year to take another step and to be more of an offensive force," said Carlyle. "To drive more of the offense from the back end. And I think he's done a heck of a job."

Won gold at the 2009 World Under-18 Championship and named best defenseman

Won gold at the 2010 World Junior Championship

Won the 2010 Memorial Cup and named to the tournament All-Star team

Played in the 2017 NHL All-Star Game

After spending the off-season focusing on improving his shot, and taking his father's advice to use a longer stick, Fowler had 11 goals and 39 points in 2016–17. He also led the Pacific Division champions in average ice time at almost 25 minutes a night and played in his first All-Star Game, while becoming "the guy that can right the ship a little bit," as he put it.

Trade rumors had surrounded Fowler all season long, but a player with his mobility, speed and poise who can play both ends of the ice and on the power play and penalty is extremely rare. With those assets, one NHL scout, who wished to remain anonymous, predicted Fowler would remain a Duck. "There's no way they're trading him. You don't trade your best defenseman if you want to keep your job."

Sure enough Ducks general manager Bob Murray inked Fowler to an eight-year, $52 million extension in the off-season, ensuring job security for both men in Anaheim.

♠ 41

MIKE SMITH

PACIFIC DIVISION | Flames | Goalie

41 ♠

goalie record-tying three assists in a game and a league-leading six assists in 2005–06.

Smith finally got a shot with the big club in Dallas in 2006–07 as a backup to Marty Turco. Again he earned a shutout in his debut, blanking the Phoenix Coyotes on October 21, 2006, to become the first goalie in franchise history with a shutout in his first game.

Smith was named to the 2006–07 All-Rookie Team and played another season in Dallas before being traded to the Tampa Bay Lightning in February 2008. In 2011, after three and a half years of fighting for the number one job, being waived and sent packing to the minors, he was signed as a free agent by the Phoenix Coyotes, who gave him the starting role.

Smith blossomed in the desert. He had 38 regular season wins, a 2.21 goals-against average, a .930 save percentage and a club record-tying eight shutouts in 2011–12. He finished fourth in Vezina Trophy voting as the Coyotes won their first division title in 33 years.

In the playoffs he backstopped the Coyotes to wins over the Chicago Blackhawks and Nashville Predators before losing to the eventual Stanley Cup champion Los Angeles Kings in the Western Conference Final. "He got to Phoenix and everything seemed to come in order, talking about his motivation, his health, his working with Sean Burke that gave him confidence in his game just to stay put, play a little bit deeper," said Turco about his former backup.

The following seasons brought a playoff drought to the Coyotes. While Smith's NHL team struggled he found solace on international ice. Named to Team Canada for the 2014 Sochi Olympics by general manager Steve Yzerman (who had waived him in Tampa), he was the third-string goalie, earning a gold medal and some validation as a member of one of the

The man knows how to make an entrance. Scoring a goal or earning a shutout in your professional debut is the dream of every player. If you do both you're either playing a video game or you're Mike Smith.

The Kingston, Ontario, native not only got a shutout in his first start for the Lexington Men O' War of the East Coast Hockey League in 2002, but he singlehandedly outscored his opponents with a goal into an empty net. There's no better possible start, but it didn't exactly fast track him to the NHL.

Selected in the fifth round of the 2001 entry draft by the Dallas Stars, Smith's long and winding road also included stops with the Utah Grizzlies, the Houston Aeros and the Iowa Stars, as well as an AHL

strongest teams the country has ever assembled. He also joined his wife, Brigitte Acton, who competed in slalom skiing, as a Canadian Olympian.

The Olympics helped Smith get the starting job for Canada at the 2015 World Championship, where he posted a 1.50 goals-against average and .930 save percentage in eight games. He also had a shutout streak of 190:03 minutes that ended during Canada's 6–1 victory in the gold medal game. "The Olympic stage is obviously a lot different, but for me to be honest, on a personal note it's more rewarding this time around just because I had more to do with it than in Sochi," said Smith after the tournament. "To be in the net for the majority of the games and to really have something to hang my hat on as far as winning, it definitely will hold a special place in my heart for a long time."

Smith missed exactly half of the 2015–16 with an injury, but the time off refocused him and he was determined to come back strong the following season. The Coyotes missed the playoffs again in 2016–17, but in his 12th NHL season, at the age of 34, Smith played in his first All-Star Game. He was the third-oldest goalie in history to make his debut, behind Johnny Bower and Manny Legace.

In 2017, after making the playoffs for just the second time in eight seasons, the resurgent Calgary Flames decided they needed an upgrade and traded for Smith in the off-season. If history is any indication, it should be a magical debut.

Named to the NHL All-Rookie Team in 2007

Tied for the NHL lead in shutouts in 2012–13

Won gold at the 2014 Olympics

Won gold at the 2015 World Championship

Played in the 2017 NHL All-Star Game

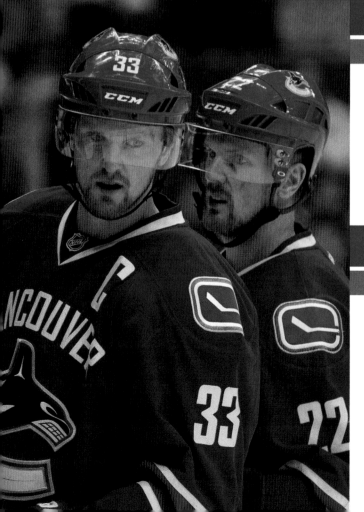

HENRIK SEDIN

PACIFIC DIVISION | Canucks | Center | 33

- Won gold at the 2006 Olympics
- Played in three NHL All-Star Games (2008, 2011, 2012)
- Won the Art Ross and Hart Trophies in 2010
- Won gold at the 2013 World Championship

DANIEL SEDIN

PACIFIC DIVISION | Canucks | Left Wing | 22

- Won gold at the 2006 Olympics and silver at the 2014 Olympics
- Played in three NHL All-Star Games (2011, 2012, 2016)
- Won the Art Ross Trophy in 2011
- Voted the Ted Lindsay Award winner in 2011
- Won gold at the 2013 World Championship

The only thing missing from Henrik Sedin's 1,000th NHL point was his brother hitting the milestone on the same goal. Daniel Sedin did assist on the goal, of course, which Henrik put past Roberto Luongo of the Florida Panthers on January 20, 2017.

Henrik, whose first NHL point came against the Panthers in his second career game in October 2000, became the first Canuck, fourth Swede and 85th player in NHL history to reach 1,000 points. It's only natural that he got there ahead of his brother. Henrik is six minutes older than Daniel, who should join him early in the 2017–18 season.

The Sedin twins were born in Ornskoldsvik, the legendary town in northern Sweden that has given the world more hockey players than its population of 29,000 would suggest. Growing up, Henrik and Daniel looked up to their two older brothers, Peter and Stefan. They let the twins tag along to the rink and their street hockey games, and the younger brothers just wanted to prove they belonged. It instilled an early competitiveness that led them to the NHL.

After moving up through the MoDo system in their hometown, which has produced Peter Forsberg, Markus Naslund and Victor Hedman, among many others, the Sedins both won the 1999 Guldpucken (Golden Puck) as Sweden's best players. It was the first and only time the award has been shared.

Then-Canucks general manager Brian Burke pulled off some transactional magic to keep the brothers together. Holding the third overall pick in 1999, he made three trades before the draft began so he could take Daniel second and Henrik third overall.

The Sedins entered the league in 2000, and since then only five players have more points than each of them does, and only Joe Thornton has more assists than Henrik. They also drove the most successful period in Canucks history, from 2003–04 to 2012–13, which included seven division titles, two Presidents' Trophies and a trip to the Stanley Cup Final in 2011.

Henrik's best year was 2009–10, when he won the Art Ross Trophy after a career high 29 goals and 112 points, while proving he could put up points without Daniel, who missed 19 games. After the season, Henrik took home the Hart Trophy as league MVP.

Spurred by a little sibling rivalry, in 2010–11 Daniel had 41 goals and 104 points to keep the Art Ross in the family, and added the Lester B. Pearson Award (now the Ted Lindsay Award) for league MVP as voted on by the players.

Hard as it is to tell them apart, on the ice and off, in simple terms Henrik sets them up and Daniel knocks them down.

Entering the 2017–18 season, Henrik was the franchise leader in games played (1,248), assists (784), points (1,021) and plus-minus (plus-187). Daniel was second in games played (1,225) and first in goals (370), even-strength goals (241), power-play goals (129), game-winning goals (81) and shots (3,285).

From 2006–07 to 2015–16, one of the Sedins led Vancouver in scoring every season, usually with the other in second. Both have passed Forsberg to become the two highest point producers from Ornskoldsvik, and they are eighth and ninth on the active NHL career points list.

Ten days before Henrik had his 1,000th point Alex Ovechkin got his, and a few weeks later Sidney Crosby joined them with four figures. That, in a nutshell, explains why the Sedins haven't always received the recognition they deserved.

Crosby and Ovechkin are surefire Hall of Famers; the Sedins are building a case. There's only one player in the post-expansion era to win the Hart Trophy and not be voted into the Hall of Fame (Jose Theodore in 2002), and since the Art Ross Trophy was first handed out in 1948, every player who earned it is now enshrined.

At 37, and entering the last year of their matching contracts in 2017–18, the Sedins are nearing the end of their magnificent and nearly identical run. When they eventually retire, they'll surely do it together.

Then, for the first time in their lives, they may not be joined at the hip. But they could be side-by-side forever at the Hall of Fame, with Daniel first — but only alphabetically.

JOE THORNTON

PACIFIC DIVISION | Sharks | Center | 19

- Named CHL and OHL Rookie of the Year in 1996

- Won gold at the 1997 World Junior Championship

- Selected first overall in the 1997 NHL entry draft

- Won gold at the World Cup of Hockey in 2004 and 2016

- Won Switzerland's National League A title in 2005

- Won silver at the 2005 World Championship

- Won the Art Ross and Hart Trophies in 2006

- Won gold at the 2010 Olympics

- Played in six NHL All-Star Games (2002, 2003, 2004, 2007, 2008, 2009)

umbo was a circus elephant that died in 1885 in St. Thomas, Ontario, when a wayward train hit him. It was the biggest story to come out of the town of 40,000 until "Jumbo" Joe Thornton, a century or so later.

It's merely a coincidence, according to Glen Murray, his teammate on the Boston Bruins, who didn't know about the four-legged St. Thomas legend when he coined Thornton's nickname. The enduring moniker is one of the few positives from Thornton's time in Beantown after the Bruins chose him first overall in the 1997 entry draft.

Thornton never fit in with the Bruins' regime at the time, and criticism of his play hit a crescendo after a seven-game loss to the Montreal Canadiens in the first round of the 2004 playoffs, even though he was playing with torn cartilage in his rib cage.

Despite putting up 454 points in 532 games with the Bruins, Thornton was traded to the San Jose Sharks in November 2005. He promptly became the first player in NHL history to win the Art Ross and Hart Trophies after being dealt mid-season. He won the scoring title with 125 points, including 96 assists, in 2005–06, the highest point total ever recorded by a player on two different teams in the same season.

Thornton led the league in assists the next two seasons, and with 92 in 2006–07 he became just the third player in history with consecutive 90 assist seasons, joining Wayne Gretzky and Mario Lemieux.

Since arriving in San Jose, Thornton has averaged more than a point a game, with 937 points in 914 games by the end of the 2016–17 season. The 6-foot-4, 220-pound center has also grown a beard worthy of a wizard of Middle-earth, befitting his position as wise old man of the West Coast.

But he's not just a mascot; Thornton still puts up numbers. In 2015–16, at 36 years old, he had 82 points in 82 games, making him one of only 14 players in history to average a point per game when they were his age or older.

With 394 goals and 1,007 assists at the conclusion of the 2016–17 season, Thornton was 13th all-time in assists and tied with Brett Hull for 22nd in points, and he's second to Jaromir Jagr in both assists and points among active players. "Honestly, I've been lucky enough to stay healthy all these years and play with a lot of good scorers," said Thornton after recording his 1,000th assist on March 6, 2017. "For a passer that's probably the key — it's just having the Jonathan Cheechoos, the Glen Murrays, the Joe Pavelskis, you know, the Patty Marleaus."

Patrick Marleau, the second overall pick in 1997 (one spot after Thornton), was Thornton's long-time Sharks teammate before signing as a free agent with the Toronto Maple Leafs in 2017. Over 19 years in San Jose, Marleau scored 508 goals and 1,082 points, both tops in franchise history. With Marleau's departure, Thornton takes over the veteran position on the Sharks.

In 2017 Thornton signed a one-year, $8 million contract to stay with the Sharks. "I feel like I've got a lot left in the tank, and hopefully after this deal I'll keep signing," said Thornton on his new contract. "But I felt comfortable with it. The team felt comfortable with it. It's that simple, I guess."

Prior to 2016 both Thornton and Marleau had the dubious distinction of being number one and two on the list of players with the most career playoff games without an appearance in the Stanley Cup Final. That was broken after the Sharks won the 2016 Western Conference title, but after losing to the Pittsburgh Penguins both are still searching for their first Cup. Thornton doesn't plan to give up that quest anytime soon.

"I'm going to play as long as I can because I love coming to the rink," he said. "I do love the guys. I like the fellowship. I just like everything about it. I'm just really passionate about the game of hockey."

For the Gandalf on skates, the only prize left for him is the fellowship of a Stanley Cup ring.

PROFILE INDEX

PHOTO CREDITS

Icon Sportswire
Adam Davis 127, 132
Allan Hamilton 144, 156
Andrew Dieb 90, 91, 98, 122, 151
Bob Frid 5, 149, 154
Carlos Herrera 78, 140
Chris Williams 121, 123, 131, 136, 147, 150
Curtis Comeau 126, 129, 134, 145
Danny Murphy 95, 97, 116
David Dennis 124
David Hahn 20, 59, 82, 113, 120, 128
David Kirouac 12, 22, 23, 24, 25, 31, 43, 54, 69, 73, 92, 135
Derek Cain 96
Fred Kfoury III 15, 28, 34
Gavin Baker 75
Gerry Angus 14, 33, 42, 143
Greg Thompson 52, 74, 111
Jason Kopinski 45
Jason Mowry 60, 79
Jeanine Leech 2–3, 6, 17, 21, 32, 48, 50, 51, 53, 56, 61, 65, 87, 88, 99, 105, 118, 125, 130, 141, 156
Jerome Davis 29
John Crouch 39, 66, 112, 114, 158
Jose Quiroz 137, 138, 142
Julian Avram 46, 85, 115
Justin Berl 49, 77, 106
Keith Gillett 101, 103
Kevin Abele 16, 152
Kyle Ross 68

Marc Sanchez 9
Mark Goldman 55, 72
Mark LoMoglio 27, 35, 40, 41, 57
Matt Cohen 46, 70
Michael Griggs 71
Michael Tureski 36, 37, 58
Nick Wosika 102, 107, 108, 109
Rick Tapia 133, 139
Rich Graessle 64, 67, 80, 81
Richard A. Whittaker 18, 44
Robin Alam 62, 86, 89, 93, 117, 118, 148
Roy K. Miller 19
Scott Grau 26, 38
Steven Alkok 146
Steven Kingsman 104
Terrence Lee 100
Tim Spyers 153
Tony Quinn 63
Vincent Ethier 30, 76, 84, 94, 110

Front cover:
Bob Frid (Burns)
Jason Kopinski (Matthews)
Jeanine Leech (Crosby)
Rich Graessle (McDavid)
Vincent Ethier (Price)

Back cover:
Danny Murphy (Subban)
David Kirouac (top)
Ric Tapia (Quick)

Associated Press
Nick Wass 10–11

ACKNOWLEDGMENTS

Grazie mille …

Christine, for her endless support.

Julie and Steve, for their wisdom and patience.

Gregory, for being Gregory.

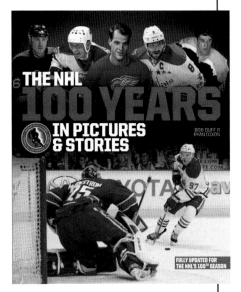
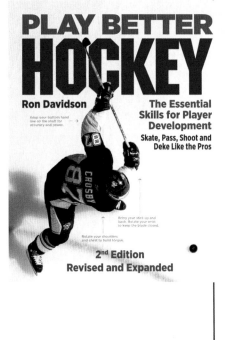